Herding Cats

The Art of Amateur Cricket Captaincy

CHARLIE CAMPBELL

BLOOMSBURY

LONDON · OXFORD · NEW YORK · NEW DELHI · SYDNEY

John Wisden & Co Ltd
An imprint of Bloomsbury Publishing Plc

50 Bedford Square
London
WC1B 3DP
UK

1385 Broadway
New York
NY 10018
USA

www.bloomsbury.com

WISDEN and the wood-engraving device are trademarks of John Wisden &
Company Ltd, a subsidiary of Bloomsbury Publishing Plc

First published 2017

www.wisden.com
www.wisdenrecords.com
Follow Wisden on Twitter @WisdenAlmanack
and on Facebook at Wisden Sports

British Library Cataloguing-in-Publication Data
A catalogue record for this book is available from the British Library.

ISBN: HB: 978-1-4729-2571-8
ePub: 978-1-4729-2573-2

2 4 6 8 10 9 7 5 3 1

Typeset in Minion by Deanta Global Publishing Services, Chennai, India
Printed and bound in Great Britain by CPI Group (UK) Ltd, Croydon CR0 4YY

To find out more about our authors and books visit www.bloomsbury.com.
Here you will find extracts, author interviews, details of forthcoming
events and the option to sign up for our newsletters.

To R

AUTHOR'S NOTE

The following is based on a true story. On a screen or page, these words are to be treated with caution. In the last eight years, I have played over 200 games of amateur cricket, for more than 20 teams, with or against over a thousand players. Some of them appear in various forms in the following pages. I hope that they will forgive me. The great majority of them have been male and so I have used "he" and "his" to refer to captains and players.

Contents

CONTENTS

CONTENTS

CONTENTS

Foreword

In an article for *The Nightwatchman* about amateur captaincy, Charlie Campbell wrote that I didn't have to deal with having nine players, and didn't have to try not to win too hard. Nor did I have a first slip suffering from a long night of ecstasy. The drug, that is. I suppose he's right: as captain I did usually have a full side of professionals, all sober and all trying to win. But Middlesex did once draw lots for a batting order in a Sunday League match. (At Cardiff, for the record. Also for the record, we won.) And I did find myself one tourist-busy August driving round Canterbury and its environs looking for a hotel for the night of a Gillette Cup quarter-final, when the match was still going on and we needed something like 16 runs to win with two wickets left. That was an evening where captaincy duties were broader than deciding whether to have three slips or two.

At Middlesex our bad memories were of a lack of hotels in Kent. Monday 17 June 1963 was the second day of the three-day match between Kent and Middlesex at Tunbridge Wells. Middlesex were in a strong position: having bowled Kent out for 150, they were 121 for three, as Peter Parfitt had been run out on 54, with Bob White not out on 43. To save money, and probably to suit the players, Middlesex had no hotel reserved for the Sunday night, Sunday being a rest day. At the start of play, at 11.30, Kent took the field under the captaincy of Colin Cowdrey. But only three Middlesex players had made it through the traffic: one a not-out batsman, one a batsman who was already out, and one the twelfth man. Kent did not offer to delay the start, and Middlesex were forced to declare. By the time Middlesex took the field, ten minutes later, they had six on the ground. They were allowed to use their twelfth man as wicketkeeper and were loaned five fielders by Kent, one of whom caught a catch. All the Middlesex team were on the field by the end of three overs. The result? Match drawn. Kent scored 341 for seven declared. Middlesex ended their second innings 82 for three, with the same not-out batsman as on Monday morning. Rain, I presume.

Here is a Fred Karno episode (now there's a dated reference, probably lost on many) that, while not quite what Charlie has had to deal with captaining the Authors XI, veers in that direction. Essex v Middlesex at Southend, 1980. Wicketkeeper Paul Downton – batting with a pulled muscle and a runner – played the ball into the covers and called for a single. Forgetting his injury (and runner), he hared off for the single. Essex lobbed the ball in to the keeper and ran him out. Should I have complained? I think not. Keith Fletcher as Essex captain was acting according to the Laws.

There may even have been a bit of history dogging this scenario. A few years earlier, we played Essex in a one-day match at Lord's. Their then-captain, Brian Taylor, was given out run out when our wicketkeeper, John Murray, had I think dropped the ball before breaking the stumps. Taylor complained and walked off in dudgeon, gesturing at me for not calling him back. I was standing near the umpire who gave him out when it happened, and I wasn't sure which was the correct decision – had Murray broken the stumps with his gloves and no ball, or had the ball itself disturbed the bails? I had no grounds for challenging his decision, but Essex were incensed. And teams, like countries, have long memories for grievances.

When I wrote *The Art of Captaincy* I set out to describe something: what the man who stood at first slip waving his arms around actually did and how it affected teams of highly skilled individuals, for better or for worse. Charlie Campbell's book explains that same process at the other end of the scale. I wish him every success. I imagine his book will be at least as relevant for captains up and down the country as mine.

Mike Brearley

Introduction

Asterisk *noun. 1. A small star-like symbol, used in writing and printing as a reference mark or to indicate omission, doubtful matter, etc.*

The asterisk is the perfect symbol for the cricket captain. Placed next to your name on the scoresheet, it indicates fallibility, unsuitable language or the need to consult another source. As you make mistakes, curse the gods and turn desperately to your team-mates for advice, you'll understand why they don't want your job. Because cricket captaincy is an almost impossible role, requiring a deep understanding of the game and, occasionally, of humanity. In no other sport can a player be selected purely for their leadership qualities. In no other sport are they so sorely needed.

Cricket is, as many have noted, only a team sport in the loosest sense. Players can quantify precisely their contribution to the overall performance. They can win while failing abjectly themselves or lose in a blaze of personal glory. Cricket's great quality is how it blends the team struggle with that of the individual. A match will be punctuated by contests between batsman and bowler, as each tries to dominate the other. But other battles are being fought, too. The captain's great challenge is to create an environment in which players celebrate the achievements of others, as well as their own: one in which the strike bowler isn't sulking as wickets fall at the other end; where the middle order aren't all willing the slow-scoring openers to get out so they can have a bat; and when players don't laugh when fielders on both sides spill catches. But how do you manage this? Most don't …

There are two principal templates for leadership in cricket. The first requires a position of almost total power. The captain should be either the best or the wealthiest player in the team – ideally both. Examples of these types include W. G. Grace, Donald Bradman and the Regency aristocrats who ran their own teams, gambling heavily on the outcome. The first two were natural cricketers for whom the role came easily and as a result they have left us little of their methodology. In his book *The Art of Cricket*, Bradman devoted more pages to running between the wickets than he did to captaincy. For him effective leadership was about dominance and averaging 99.94 in Tests. If he played well, his side was going to be hard to beat. The Australian way has always been to pick your strongest side and then choose a captain.

The second approach to cricket captaincy is epitomised by Mike Brearley who famously steered England to victory in the 1981 Ashes. Unlike Bradman, he led from the rear – his record as captain (won 17, lost four of his 31 matches in charge) was much better than his performance with the bat (no centuries in 39 Tests and an average just under 23). But through brilliant man management he turned around an England team that had been in disarray under the captaincy of Ian Botham. The best players don't always make the best leaders and Botham was just one of many who ended up failing at the role. Brearley may not always have been among the top 11 players in England but his leadership skills outweighed this. In his classic book, *The Art of Captaincy*, he quotes Xenophon, who wrote that an elected general should be "ingenious, energetic, careful, full of stamina and presence of mind ... loving and tough, straightforward and crafty, ready to gamble everything and wishing to have everything, generous and greedy, trusting and suspicious". He considers that Xenophon had it about right.

But if, as Brearley's title suggests, leading a professional cricket team is an art, what of the amateur captain? Is this role also an art? Could it even be a science? And what else is different? We know about the great captains of the international game and there have been many fine leaders in first-class cricket. At the pinnacle of the sport, their job is to win. They have no wider duty to the game. But what about the layer of captains beneath them? Who are the legendary skippers of the amateur game? We don't hear about those who've led their league team for decades, up and down the divisions. Extracting the best out of a side of highly motivated and skilled sportsmen is not easy. But how much harder is captaincy lower down? The job is no longer solely about winning. You are like one of those fish that lives on the seabed, developing ways of coping with the intense pressure and lack of light hundreds of metres below the surface. In the cricketing abyss, you struggle to keep hold of your players in the sludge and darkness. Not because other teams are trying to poach them, but because there are other demands on their time. Work and family don't mix well with a game that takes up a whole day. You won't have the professionals' facilities or backroom support either. And you will be dealing with players who lack both cricketing sense and ability. They will often be manifestly unfit, maybe even the worse for wear from the previous night's excesses. They will also often be in a state of complete despair about their own game but unwilling to take the steps necessary to improve, like practice. They will have a range of inventive excuses for their failures – usually each other, but once it was flat-hunting that caused a batsman's dismissal. Nor will there always be 11 of you – late drop-outs are inevitable in amateur cricket. Often the 11th player is the child of the tenth and the tenth the son of the ninth. If this is all sounding a little biblical, that should be no surprise. Cricket has long been held up by some as a religion, or at the very least a cult, with its strange rituals and outfits.

Cricket has many of the trappings of faith. The first record of cricket as an adult activity was at the prosecution of two men in 1611 for playing when they should have been in church. Derek Birley's *A Social*

History of English Cricket also recounts how Maidstone was considered "a very prophane town", which saw "Morrice Dancing, Cudgels, Stoolball, Crickets" on the Sabbath. George Bernard Shaw famously wrote that "the English are not a very spiritual people, so they invented cricket to give them an idea of eternity". For many of us it is as close as we get to belief. The sport has its own special book, *Wisden Cricketers' Almanack*, and, like the ancient Mayans, its own immensely complicated calendar. There is a priestly class, the keepers of the flame, in the form of MCC, who administer the game's Laws. Most sports merely have rules. Such is the premium it places on experience and wisdom that applicants must wait 27 years before being able to join. Worshippers flock to Lord's, the Home of Cricket, to pay homage to the game. They can buy indulgences – in the form of merchandise from the Lord's shop – before marvelling at the relics that are housed in the MCC museum. These range from the Ashes urn and Bradman's boots to Denis Compton's kneecap. Cricket even had its own schism, as power moved east and India and Twenty20 started to dominate.

Ancient laws, rituals, burnt offerings, infallible officials, a reformation … cricket has all of these. Like many belief systems, it harks constantly back to a better, purer time, before the game was corrupted by money. The struggle between the traditionalists and the modernisers is a constant one and has been raging since the game's very beginning. There must have been opposition to the introduction of the third stump, just as there was to the emergence of roundarm and overarm bowling and the invention of DRS. Each side interprets the spirit of cricket in their own way. Many embrace the changes that have come as the sport has been adopted by other countries. If the class barriers have not come down completely, they have at least been lowered, and women are at long last encouraged to play. But there are some who wish the sport could be more like golf.

A cricketing Eden never existed and money has always been at the heart of the game but there are many who continue to practise the old ways, playing as we imagine it was once played, purely for the sake of it. This could be on the traditional English village green but the game now belongs as much on the maidan in Mumbai, or in a street in Karachi with a tapeball. What do the participants there care of edicts from St John's Wood? The only numbers that matter are those in the scorebook. They are not businesspeople trying to improve on last year's statistics. They are playing this game for the sheer enjoyment of it. This strand of the amateur game is more like a pagan cult than a religion – ancient, earthier and unchanged by time. At the head of this cult is one person – the captain.

An amateur captain may have a great many more responsibilities than in other sports but with them comes the power to play however you want. You can choose your opposition, without the interference of any administrators above you. You can choose where you play. You can choose the format. (My team, the Authors, has played T20s, two-innings games over two days and everything in between.) You can even make your own rules. There is at least one side that doesn't allow players to be out first ball. On the field, your word is law. (Well, most of the time.) If your opening bowler is bowling too short too often at a helmetless batsman on a spicy pitch you can take him off. If your middle-order batsmen are too quick to shut up shop and block out for a draw, you can give instructions to force the pace. If that fails, you can send a new umpire out with instructions to raise the finger the next time the bowler clears his throat. If your keeper and slip cordon chirp too aggressively at the new batsman, they'll be fielding on the boundary the next game. If they're playing, that is.

The amateur captain has dubious antecedents in the form of the Regency aristocrats, a degenerate bunch who organised matches against each other, and employed cricketers on their estates for this purpose. Huge sums were staked on the outcome of these games and so the best players were sought. Edward "Lumpy" Stevens, the greatest bowler of his age, worked for the Earl of Tankerville as a gardener and many other outstanding cricketers found jobs in this way. A scorecard from the time was a curious sight, with the bulk of the runs seemingly coming from the tail. Players were listed by social rank, with the aristocrats eking out a few runs at the top and the professionals making hundreds at nine, ten and 11.

Since then a new template for amateur cricket has emerged. The captain no longer owns the ground upon which the game is played. Nor are the best players dependent on him for their livelihood. The game has broadened and there are now thousands of cricket clubs, from those registered with the ECB that put out five teams on a Saturday and two on a Sunday to the village XIs who play their local rivals and friendlies against wandering sides. England is liberally stocked with beautiful grounds. In some counties it feels as if every village has one. A Sunday match played on the green is, for many, the perfect incarnation of the summer game. And while the professional game has been revolutionised over the last hundred years, the village game remains the same, or so we like to think.

Those who have written about it tend to peddle the same bucolic vision. A thatched pub squats at the boundary's edge, out of which spill garrulous bearded locals, tankards in hand. On the pitch, the players are getting on with the game. They are either incredibly good or incredibly bad, nothing in between. Balls are hit for six or flatten the stumps. There are no uneventful moments, none of those longueurs that cricket specialises in. The blacksmith roars up the hill to bowl, while the vicar sends down his gentle lobs from the other end. A child fields at backstop and a stockbroker, who has recently moved to the village, is out for nought. Ducks waddle past the boundary rope. The umpire is drunk and makes a number of poor decisions. An American is playing the game for the first time and cannot make sense of it all. And so on. It is a timeless scene and a lovely one. A. G. Macdonell captured all this in *England, Their England* and Hugh de Selincourt in *The Cricket Match* but there are echoes of it elsewhere.

These writers could have been describing J. M. Barrie who did all of this for real. He possessed tremendous enthusiasm and very little skill. The greats – Bradman, Sobers, Tendulkar – are always described as natural cricketers. Barrie was their polar opposite. There are players whose every movement betrays how hard they find the sport. Running, catching and throwing are deeply unnatural to them; the techniques of bowling and batting even more alien. Onlookers express surprise that they don't fall over more frequently. But there they are, playing most weekends, defying the laws of physics. Barrie's gifts were mostly deployed off the field. He ran his team, the Allahakbarries, with charm and energy and represented a third way of captaincy. He founded his side because no other would have him, like many have since. In the Allahakbarries, it was acceptable to be hopeless, if not actively encouraged. Barrie was a slow bowler himself and said that after a delivery he would go to mid-off and sit there, waiting for the ball to reach the other end. Sometimes it did and sometimes it didn't. If he didn't like the delivery, he'd run after it and stop it before it could reach the other end. The story of his team is delightfully recounted in Kevin Telfer's *Peter Pan's First XI* and the Allahakbarries inspired a type of cricket that continues to this day.

J. M. Barrie also played for another wandering side from the same period, one that I have captained for the last five years. The Authors' Club was founded in 1891 and its cricket side featured Arthur Conan Doyle, A. A. Milne and P. G. Wodehouse. Each year, they took on the Actors or Publishers at Lord's, though Barrie didn't make the cut for these games. On one occasion Conan Doyle and Wodehouse opened the batting together. Conan Doyle was a solid cricketer, playing ten first-class matches for MCC. (His highest score was 43 and he took one wicket, that of W. G. Grace himself.) Wodehouse was then an emerging novelist and a fast bowler fresh out of the Dulwich First XI. The Actors were captained by the formidably mustachioed C. Aubrey Smith. The star of films like *The Prisoner of Zenda* and *Little Lord Fauntleroy*, Smith was an excellent cricketer, nicknamed "Round the Corner" for his unusual curving run-up. He played for Cambridge, MCC, Transvaal and Sussex and represented England in one Test, in which he took five wickets. He later moved to Los Angeles, where he launched the Hollywood Cricket Club, with Wodehouse as secretary and Boris Karloff behind the stumps.

A later incarnation of the Authors was captained by Douglas Jardine and featured some of the greatest players in history – Denis Compton, Richie Benaud and Jack Fingleton – with a handful of novelists and poets making up the tail. This literary Lashings had lost its ties with the original Authors' Club in Whitehall and played each year against the National Book League in Westminster's Vincent Square. The side re-emerged briefly in the 1980s before petering out once again. Proper teams have committees and structures to ensure longevity and succession. Sides like the Authors usually depend on the lunatic enthusiasm of one person, which is why they die out, re-emerge and die out again. I've played for dozens of similar teams and it's always the same.

In September 2011, the Authors were revived in unpromising surroundings. I sat in a car with Nicholas Hogg, a novelist and former Leicestershire Under-19 cricketer. We had just played the last league match of the season in the shadow of the M25 as power lines crackled overhead. A bleak cricketless winter stretched before us. In a bid to alleviate this despair we talked about next season. A few weeks before we'd put together a team of writers for a one-off match in Kent. Could we do so again? Quite quickly we were planning the perfect summer of cricket and the recruiting started. A few years previously, I'd started playing for the historian Tom

Holland's Sunday team, after a decade-long absence from the game. The standard was pleasingly low and the conversation ridiculously erudite. A number of the team were writers and in this company I was able to scramble a few runs and even take two wickets. I hadn't known cricket like this existed. At school I'd been a weak player, dropping five catches the one time I was selected for a team. The ball followed me mercilessly that afternoon and I made a duck to boot.

So I wasn't the obvious choice to captain this new team but Nick didn't want to, and nor did anyone else. Like Barrie, and hundreds of others in Sunday cricket, I found myself in charge, playing a sport I hadn't quite mastered. Soon there were others. Tom joined, along with Jon Hotten, whose Old Batsman blog I'd long admired, and children's author Anthony McGowan. Nick, Jon and Tony were all fine cricketers in their youth, with varying degrees of reticence about their feats. Tom was a good and strangely effective bowler, if prone to dropping the simplest catches. These four became the stalwarts of the side, playing each week, on the council pitch in Hackney where we started and the more scenic grounds that followed. In our first five seasons together, we played almost 150 matches and I had some of the most enriching experiences of my life. After a certain age, many of us find that we no longer make friends in the way that we used to when young. Writers enter the world of books thinking they've finally found their people. But these people spend most of their time in a room on their own. There are few mechanisms for them to spend much time together enjoyably, where they don't find themselves comparing careers. A cricket team proved to be a surprisingly successful way of doing this and provides the right element of competition.

Nick, Tom, Tony, Jon and I were joined by a dozen others. Somehow we've played on a number of Test grounds, on Mumbai's maidans and in the Rajasthan desert, in Sri Lanka's tea country and on grounds rebuilt after the 2004 tsunami, as well as on pitches the length and breadth of England. We have faced opposition that has included the national team of Japan, a Rajasthan Royals XI and the Vatican. We have been dismantled by sides much better than us and have somehow triumphed against others whom we'd never expected to beat. We've been dismissed and hit for six by countless former professional players. But just occasionally we've come out on top against them. We've lost seven straight games and narrowly avoided mutiny during that run. But we've won a great many matches, too, despite a selection policy that requires players to have had a book published. It's been a steep learning curve for all, particularly for a novice captain.

Cricket asks a lot of those who play it. It is a game of great complexity and there are so many ways in which things can go wrong. Just look at how it punishes those who are playing together for the first time. When the Authors first took the field, we put in a horrible ragged performance on a wet concrete pitch in Hackney. Catches went down, extras flowed and at least one player broke his glasses in the field, cursing a nonexistent groundsman. That day we relied entirely on individuals, rather than teamwork. Few could take any pride in our performance. Our first-ever wicket was a stumping off a wide – a moment of brilliance from one player making up for the failure of another. Our opening batsman Sam kept us in the hunt, as we sheltered under a tree, before the rain became heavier. But something happened that day, enough to keep us coming back. Cricket is like that. It gives you enough to keep going, when you most need it. After five years of playing together, we are far from perfect and will put in at least one shocking performance every season. But we're a world away from that fumbling XI that would lose and lose and lose again. Some of this is down to captaincy, some down to time spent together.

We're well-drilled in the field and mostly stand in the right places. We know our weaknesses, as well as our strengths. We know when we have to back up a hard throw and when we have to run towards the fielder because he can only underarm the ball back from the boundary.

Recently we played a team much like we were then. Just as we had, they'd bluffed their way onto various lovely grounds, only to come unstuck upon them. That is the natural order of things. Good pitches are made for good cricketers. The groundsman doesn't spend hours preparing a track for a bowler who can't hit it. It pains him to see wides and no-balls and misfields on his immaculate turf, where greater players have trod and will tread again. That day we put the pretenders to the sword, running up a score of 296 in 40 overs. We weren't unusually strong: they were dreadful. The 11th man was late so I fielded for them for the first dozen overs and was able to see them up close.

Their bowlers were short of practice and probably quality, too. Only one of them, the captain, showed any kind of consistency. The rest of them served up several bad balls an over. My childhood hero Waqar Younis was feared by batsmen for his toe-crunching yorkers. Their third-change almost broke his own toe, releasing the ball straight into the ground beneath him, not once but twice. And yet he continued to bowl. Their skipper had no other options. We've all had those despairing moments, when there is no one you can trust with the ball. You know you have to find eight overs from somewhere. Do you ask an occasional spinner, knowing he'll concede at least 60 runs? Do you take the gloves yourself and ask the keeper to have a bowl? Dare you try the newcomer?

When it was their turn to bat, only two of their players reached double figures. Five made ducks. I'd taken the first three wickets and didn't want to come off – I guessed what was to come and the non-captain part of me wanted the glory myself. I've never taken five wickets for the team and this was as good an opportunity as I'd get. A brief internal struggle ensued. It's hard enough to get five wickets in Sunday cricket, when you usually only have seven or eight overs in which to get them. It's even harder if you're captain and have to think about the team. If I kept myself on, then others wouldn't get a game. Eventually I did the right thing and brought on our left-arm spinner. He took a wicket with his first ball, three more in that over, and finished with five for 18, as we bowled them out for 102 before the drinks break. The only resistance came from their skipper, who'd bowled so well. He made a half-century but couldn't stave off a heavy defeat. But the chasm between the teams was not as much about skill as about time spent together. We'd played together 150 times and been on five tours abroad. For the other side, this was their fourth fixture. Their branded whites and caps couldn't disguise their rawness. Nor could their hastily bestowed nicknames.

Cricket is like poker in that you scrutinise the opposition for the faintest sign of weakness. We've all been misled by a player's appearance. I've seen a 12-year-old throw down the stumps from midwicket, a morbidly obese number seven hit a quick-fire 80 and a 70-year-old seamer bowl a miserly ten-over spell. But usually appearances aren't deceptive. There are hundreds of ways in which you can spot a novice cricketer. As Shakespeare put it, "The apparel oft proclaims the man". In cricket this means that there is always a single to the man in black trainers and at least two to the fielder in chinos. Sunglasses usually denote either a very good or very weak player. The latter if they're in any way fashionable. Other tells include struggling to return the ball to the bowler each time and constant drifting out of position in the field. Amateur cricketers often do things we've seen good cricketers do on TV. We shout "catch it" when the ball goes up in the air, as if that is really going to help a weak and nervous fielder under the high ball, or "bowler", as he gathers and throws, always to the wrong end, where the batsman has comfortably made his ground. We mean to be helpful but it just doesn't work at our level. We set fields with slips and gullies to a bowler who cannot put two balls in the same spot, let alone a set of six. We either pay no attention to the state of the ball or far too much, with each player slobbering on a different side, then trying ineffectually to shine it.

That day our opposition were guilty of many of these. One player seemed to delight in throwing the ball back to the bowler as hard as he could, stinging the hands of the next fielder. By the 30th over, their team had given up. No one knew or cared where they were meant to be. The tea interval couldn't come quickly enough, nor the end. They shook our hands ruefully afterwards, before heading to the pub, where all games should end. The point of this is not to glory over a beaten foe – God knows we've been on the receiving end of hammerings enough times – but it is a useful starting point to analyse the differences between the sides, and show where a captain can make the difference, both in the short and long term.

Let's return to the three types of captaincy, as represented by Bradman, Brearley and Barrie. Brearley was unquestionably the best skipper of the three and his *The Art of Captaincy* a superb insight into his leadership of the Middlesex and England sides. In the literature on the amateur game, we have mostly heard from the Barries. Their books are often hilarious as they glory in the ineptitude of their sides. But they never seem to improve. How would Brearley tackle this type of cricket? How would he make his side better? Somehow he'd harness the star league all-rounder to the man in orange shorts who was brought in at very short notice and coax them to play together effectively. But what would he do when his best bowler was driven for six off the first ball of a match? How would he handle an over which went for 37 runs? Where would he place the fielder who can't throw, the one who can't catch, and the one who takes his phone, pint and cigarettes onto the pitch? And how would he make sure his players turned up on time?

This is what I wanted to know, convinced that therein lay the secrets to great captaincy. Ideally I'd persuade Brearley to dust off his whites and take the field again. Instead I have gone back to his book and its structure and taken inspiration from the questions he poses in it.

In each of them, surely, there is a formula for amateur captaincy. By considering them carefully, we might not scale the same heights as his teams did, but we would hopefully improve. And what more can the amateur ask for?

Captaincy in Action

It's a beautiful summer's day. A man stands alone outside a thatched pavilion watching a game of cricket. He is wearing whites, telling you he is not a spectator. (Though why would there be spectators at this out-of-the-way ground?) He's looking at the batsmen out in the middle, who are making slow progress, as the scoreboard testifies. The scorer is marking each dot ball diligently in the book. But where is the rest of the side? You scan the outfield. One is umpiring at square leg. He stands there in a white coat, hoping not to be called upon to make a decision by the fielding side against his own team-mates. Another two are walking slowly around the boundary, deep in conversation about their love lives. They are the opening batsmen, Sam and Will, dismissed cheaply early on. Cricket could not be further from their minds. High on a bank above them sits another cricketer. Nick is the team's vice-captain. No one quite knows what he is doing up there on his own – also thinking about his love life? Meditating? Learning Japanese? Being English, his team-mates never ask. They're used to these absences. In another corner of the field stands Tom, probably the most successful member of today's side. He is on the phone to Radio 4, who want his opinion on the Islamic State's latest atrocity. Towards the end of the game a taxi may arrive, to whisk him off to a studio somewhere for another opinion or two. Again, cricket is not at the forefront of his mind. Another player has gone for a walk with his family who have grown mutinous at the prospect of this whole day of cricket. It is not clear if they are coming back. Their discarded newspapers and toys lie on a picnic rug in front of the pavilion. The remaining two players are in the changing room, padding up. One will be prone, felled by a hangover. The other will be fussing over his kit, both almost entirely ignorant of the match situation. Only the captain is watching what is going on the field of play. Soon the time will come when he has to think about his own performance, like any other player, as he walks out to bat. But now he's plotting how his team can win that afternoon.

How does a captain think?

"How should he think?" Brearley asks. The amateur captain has a great deal to ponder. First you're thinking more prosaically – the what, rather than the how. The country's hopes may not be riding on what happens on this field of play but you nonetheless have your preparations to make. Unlike today's professional skipper, you are burdened with endless administrative duties in the days before a game, from selecting the team, replacing those who dropped out during the week, providing detailed directions to the ground and then driving a number of them there yourself. You may have had to shop for and make tea – these days you'll probably have to provide vegetarian or gluten-free options – before loading the car with the paraphernalia of Sunday cricket and the items certain players left behind at the last game. Only once this is all done can you focus your thoughts on your principal role, that of on-field captain. In this, your aim is to make cricket into as much of a team sport as it can be.

The footballer Steve Archibald famously defined team spirit as "an illusion only glimpsed in victory". It's a fabulous line but doesn't apply to cricket, where the best games are those in which your team fights together, in victory or defeat. Every single contribution matters. The opener makes eight runs against superb bowling, knowing that he has allowed the middle order to attack afterwards. The seamers give nothing away, as the fielders chase down every ball, as if they'd bowled it themselves. The spinners keep the pressure on and catches are all taken. Our best wins have all been like that, games in which it is hard to single out a particular player who stood out above the rest. Team spirit is forged in the heat of adversity, with shared horror stories bringing the group together. Then it cools and strengthens as the team improves.

When a captain gets it right, cricket is the best of all games, bringing people together like no other. It could be the tailender giving the set batsman the strike, at the end of a testing run chase, allowing him to make a well-deserved century; or fielders chasing down the ball after a rare bad delivery from their star bowler; or a sensational diving catch to remove the batsman who was threatening to take the game away. Moments such as these bind sportsmen like few others and even the weakest player can feel that he made a vital contribution to the side's fortunes. The captain seeks to minimise the tension between the overall performance and that of the individual as much as possible, ensuring that everyone has a role to play. The further the gap in performance between the best and worst, the less happy a team is. (It is no surprise that left-wingers like George Orwell and Harold Pinter loved cricket.) But a skipper is unlikely to be able to field a team of exactly the same ability – and why would he? Part of cricket's charm is that there should be room for everyone: the stolid opening batsman who can't hit it off the square; the spin bowler who doesn't actually turn the ball, relying instead on batsmen's folly to bring his wickets; and the specialist fielder, who isn't terribly good at that side of the game either.

But how does a captain win with these players? If we look at other sports, there are those that are "strong link", in that the team with the best player will usually win. Basketball is an example of this. Football, despite its obsession with marquee players, isn't, as the international careers of players like George Best and Ryan Giggs show. (Neither ever played at a major championship, with Northern Ireland or Wales respectively.) It is more of a "weak link" sport, in that if your team's worst three players are better than the opposition's worst three then you will tend to come out on top. Rugby is an even better example of this. Cricket falls somewhere between the two definitions but a team in which the talent range is narrow is unquestionably easier to manage than one in which you have both very strong and weak players.

The wider the gap in ability between players, the harder the captain's role becomes. The game becomes like chess. You match your best players up against the opposition's strongest and the weaker ones can battle it out. The queen should not scythe down the pawns before they've had a chance to advance into the other half of the board. It should be held in check by the other queen and rooks. When a poor batsman walks out to the middle for the opposition, and doesn't even ask for a guard, nor holds his bat properly, what do you do? You know that the first straight ball will get him. But who should bowl it? Ideally your strike bowler will bowl a foot outside off stump for the rest of the over, so the honest trundler at the other end can get his first wicket of the season. It rarely happens like that, particularly when the other batsman is trying to farm the strike against the weaker bowling. But I'll trot over to Nick at cover to discuss how to deal with the weaker batsman, just as I would with a more gifted player.

An amateur captain's perfect day is not one in which his side wins effortlessly and each stratagem works. It is the game in which every single member of his team contributes, ideally towards a narrow victory. I remember one game like this, on a sunny day in June. It was the highlight of our season, being the game against the Actors on the Nursery Ground at Lord's. Selection had been tricky – all those players mysteriously unavailable all season had suddenly got in touch to say that, yes, they could play in this particular match and were ready to bat at four and bowl first-change. But you don't drop your two top-order batsmen who've played every single game, even if their combined age is 102, and they're involved in 80 per cent of the team's run-outs. Likewise your slip stays in the team, though he will need two knee replacements at the end of the season. And you keep the change bowler who recently took his first catch in 15 years. After all, someone needs to bat at 11. So the lobbying proved futile and the strong newcomers stayed on the sidelines.

Happiness writes white, as many have said. The matches where everything goes wrong are probably more interesting to recount. So I'll be brief. That day there was no single hero. No centuries, no five-wicket hauls, just good cricket as a team. The sun blazed down and everyone did something, with the runs, wickets and catches being shared about. Bowlers kept it tight, until the batsmen wilted under the pressure and hit out. The fielders took the catches in the deep and didn't lose heart when one batsman kept depositing the ball on the roof of the indoor school. Eventually we got him when he skied one to long-off. When it was our turn to bat, the openers built a platform, blunting the opposition's attack; the middle order accelerated when needed; and the lower order hit that flurry of boundaries at the end to remove all doubt. Afterwards we stayed by the side of the pitch for hours, happily drinking and dissecting the game. If we'd had a team song, no doubt we'd have sung it, like the Australians. One player was so exhilarated by the day that he left his entire kitbag in the changing room for me to lug home.

It is only after the game that the captain can completely switch off. It may seem that you are spending the afternoon doing the same thing as the rest of your team but you stand out in that you have to concentrate, to think the whole time. For the rest of your team the game is a much-needed break from the trials of modern life. Players leave their children at home, switch their phones off and can focus on an afternoon of daydreaming and the occasional chase to the boundary. But as skipper you have much to ponder. Because in cricket things are usually about to go wrong. If they already are, you will be thinking how you should be rotating your bowlers and what field you should be setting to the batsmen. You'll be asking yourself if they have any weaknesses that can be exploited. What type of bowling would they most and least like to be facing? And when will this agony all be over?

Even when the game is going well and the wickets are falling steadily, the captain will still be fretting. Will the match finish too quickly? Will everyone get a game of sorts? Is now the time to bring on your worst bowler? Can you get away with a few overs of complete filth? If your team bowls the opposition out for under a hundred, unless you reverse the order you may well find that eight of your team don't get a bat. And that, as much as defeat, is what you dread. The Sunday captain wants to win while involving the whole team, even the useless ones. Many have struggled with the double-think involved here. How to reconcile these opposing ideas is where the true art of amateur captaincy lies.

What makes it hard for a captain to think?

Captaincy in both the professional and amateur games involves a balance of on- and off-field decisions and duties. It's when they combine that it is hardest to think sensibly. You hope that when you walk across the boundary rope you won't have to worry about anything other than the match ahead. Before a game the England skipper might have to deal with the world press, answering questions about selection and what he'll do if he wins the toss. But Alastair Cook has been trained to deal with this almost without having to engage his brain. He can talk mindlessly of the team hitting straps and executing skills, and of good areas, all while focusing on the game ahead – his tactics and own performance. And the journalists stay on the right side of the boundary rope. A Sunday captain's concerns are more prosaic, however. You'll be fretting more about the safe arrival of all 11 players – and the tea – rather than thinking of how you'll deploy them on the field.

A couple of seasons ago, we were playing the Vatican's cricket team. This was a first for us obviously – our fixture list doesn't usually include teams representing the world's largest religions. St Peter's CC had come over to play the Church of England in a historic game at Canterbury and we were lucky enough to bag one of their warm-up fixtures. The competition for places was high. We were playing at a beautiful National Trust house outside London and I arrived in good time to find a large coach already at the ground, with an ominously fit-looking team filing out of it and into the changing room. Not only was the Vatican side there on time, but they were smartly dressed in *Wisden*-yellow jackets. The team was comprised of ten young seminarians from India, Pakistan and Sri Lanka, training for the priesthood in Rome, and was led by an English priest, Father Tony Currer. As I chatted to my opposite number, I spied Tom wandering around the outfield. We were due to start in half an hour and at the moment were playing two versus 11. A text message came in announcing that five team-mates were in the pub having lunch. (Four of them claimed that the fifth had ordered a sizeable feast and they were waiting for his food to turn up. And the first pub they'd been due to meet in had been shut for several years.) The remaining players were en route, held up by what they described as the complete closure of the same motorway we'd driven up just a few minutes earlier. Meanwhile, the opposition started to warm up on the outfield, doing shuttle runs and other strenuous exercises. But you can't intimidate an opposition if nine of them aren't there.

There are many nightmare scenarios for the amateur captain and one of the worst is walking out for the toss without everyone from your team there. If you call correctly, you must choose to bat, or field without the full complement. If you lose the toss you must throw yourself at the opposition's mercy. Their captain might be generous, having been in this position himself. They might suggest delaying the start time by 15 minutes or lend you a fielder or two. If they had been in two minds over whether to bat first or not, they might even let your predicament sway them towards fielding first. But they will be judging you. There is no better test of the health of an amateur cricket club than the time the players turn up. Amateur captains are perfectly used to starting or finishing a game without 11. Brearley never had to deal with Botham leaving early to get to a party somewhere, nor the top order arriving late because traffic was bad and both Boycott and Tavaré had driven too slowly and dallied in the service station.

As we walked out onto the pitch, I could see five sheepish figures hurrying past the pavilion and into the changing room at the side. This was the contingent from the pub, back from lunch. We were now seven and my phone was buzzing with traffic updates and apologies. I won the toss and paused. The obvious option was to bat first but I thought again and chose to field. I had a number of reasons for wanting to chase – I was pretty sure we were playing a stronger side and when your top-order batsmen are not known for scoring quickly, sometimes it is better if they know what's required. There was also an unworthy part of me that wanted to make a statement. That wanted to tell those players just how much they'd let me down. If a latecomer sidles into the changing room as the middle order is padding up, he heaves a sigh of relief, mumbles an apology and accepts his demotion down the order. But running out onto the field, several overs in, he knows he's let his entire team down.

In football it is commonly said a team played better with ten men, after one was sent off. That day, we played heroically with just seven on the field. Our bowlers knew there was no room for error and kept a good line and length. Meanwhile, the fielders covered every scrap of ground – with only three fielders on one side and two on the other, we were a blur of perpetual motion. With only six team-mates, almost every ball might be yours to retrieve. One by one, the four missing players trickled on. But so much for making a statement. Three were suitably contrite but one didn't realise he'd missed the first six overs. He ran on at the end of the over, thinking we'd just started and that he'd timed it perfectly, missing that boring warm-up. If he was surprised they only batted for 24 overs, while we had 30, he didn't show it. I had to explain it to him afterwards through gritted teeth.

We lost on the final ball. A boundary would have won it for us but Peter, our former Croatian international, couldn't quite bisect the men on the rope. A game that had begun badly ended thrillingly and everything was forgiven, if not forgotten. Afterwards our opposition invited us to pray with them. As we bowed our heads in front of the pavilion, our thoughts turned to God's infinite mercy.

Choosing a Captain

No amateur captain needs an ECB survey to tell them what they already know – that playing numbers are in decline. You face an incredible struggle to get a team out each week. The last game of the season is always the most important one for the amateur skipper. By then, up to half of your players will be deciding whether to play next year, whether they'll put up with the aches, strains and (marital) strife that a full summer of cricket entails. A decent team performance can erase untold painful memories from earlier in the season and a good individual one will banish all winter's doubts. You just have to coax enough runs or wickets from those players to ensure you have a full team next year.

This is not a problem that the professional captain faces. Those at the pinnacle of the game can choose from the country's 844,000 active cricketers – though realistically, only the last 1,000 are in the running. The remaining 843,000 of us are making up the numbers. And despite these numbers, many amateur skippers will struggle to put out a full side every weekend.

It is perfectly normal for players to drop out on the eve or morning of a match. If this happens in Saturday league cricket, the first team takes the seconds' star all-rounder but will bat him at ten and not bowl him. The seconds will plunder the thirds for their best batsman and probably won't give him back. The thirds will reluctantly borrow someone from the fourths, hoping he won't let them down too much. And the fourths will be short, again, and may have to find something else to do that afternoon.

The role of the Sunday captain is harder. A few hundred years ago he would have been patrolling the taverns in a seaside town, pressganging unwary drinkers into going to sea. At risk were "eligible men of seafaring habits between the ages of 18 and 55 years". The amateur captain is not in a position to be so fussy. I've recruited a number of players the night before a game, having never seen them play. I've found players using social media, at weddings, even once in the lift of our hotel. Other people make small talk, I cut straight to the chase. "Do you play cricket?" I ask. "What are you doing tomorrow?" On tour in India I recruited our waiter during breakfast. He took two steepling catches at long-on. At a game in the New Forest I enlisted the sole spectator – lending him the spare whites I always bring – and he duly lost us the game with the one over he bowled. Captaincy requires this heady mix of desperation and optimism. Everyone you meet is a possible convert. In the face of this struggle, you wonder why anyone would *want* to be captain.

Why do so many players want to be captain?

When playing cricket it is very hard not to captain in your head. Just as some people press an imaginary brake pedal when in a car's passenger seat, so the amateur cricketer is making mental adjustments to the captain's field. Imagine there were thought bubbles above each fielder, during a match. You would see that not all of them will be thinking about cricket obviously. It is a fielder's right to daydream after all. But the thoughts of those focused on the game won't be flattering. A number will be disagreeing with you and they may well be right. They'll have seen that it's time to make that bowling change, move square leg five steps in and wake midwicket up. Often they won't say anything and will let you get on with your job. But when three shots have gone through a particular gap and still you haven't plugged it, then one of them will trot over and gently suggest what everyone's thinking.

There's no doubt that it's easier to captain when you're not actually in charge. You remember all the times you're right and few of those when you weren't. Your decisions and instincts aren't held up to scrutiny, nor proved wrong. In real time, if you move a fielder, a good batsman often places the ball in the gap you just created. That doesn't happen if you're captaining in your head. What many players would settle for is being able to decide when they get to bat and bowl. And maybe setting the field when they're bowling. That's why you're there, after all. Never mind the rest. Who gives up a whole day at the weekend to stand at mid-off and tinker with field placings, over by over, without any lapse in concentration for the entire innings? No, the fun is to be had in the middle, timing the ball all around the park, fielders following it to the boundary; or with ball in hand, making it go one way or another, before sending the batsman back to the pavilion, your name next to his in the scorebook. Who really enjoys standing around for 40 overs? Relatively few of us. The first hour is often fun and the last five overs can be tense. But those in the middle ... If you look around the field after 25 overs, the players' body language will tell you everything about their state of mind. They are no longer walking in purposefully, ready for the ball to come to them. Square leg will be talking to the umpire, long-off will be sitting on a bench by the sightscreen and third man will be checking the Test score on his mobile phone.

There are worse things for a captain than your team-mates' lack of concentration, though. It is almost inevitable that a couple of your players will be sulking at any one time, usually because they don't feel sufficiently involved in the game. Ideally you should ensure that one is on the off side and the other on the leg, in case they start to conspire. They may be angry with you, sometimes with each other. The obvious way to stop a player from moping around in the field is to let him bowl. But usually he's cross because you'd taken him off after a particularly erratic spell and you just can't afford to bring him back on for a second go. It's too dangerous. So instead you summon him from the deep and place him where he'll be more involved, at risk even, under the batsman's nose. There is nothing like the prospect of injury and heroism to lift the spirits.

Just occasionally, a player will do more than sulk. It is hard watching your team slide to defeat without wanting to do something about it. On one such occasion I found myself deposed as on-field captain. One moment I was in charge, the next I was the one sulking on the boundary as we lost our heads. Team spirit is always harder to maintain when abroad, as many touring sides have shown over the years. Players are cooped up with each other in a way that doesn't happen at home. Tired and in unfamiliar surroundings, they can squabble over the smallest things. In this match we were playing in India under lights on a pitch next to Mumbai airport. We'd stood in English rain countless times but this was our first experience of the dew factor and we coped no better with these damp conditions. We batted first and ran up a good score, passing 200 in our 30 overs. By the time we took the field for the second innings, the dew had soaked the grass and our bowlers and fielders struggled against a very strong batting line-up. Few of our seamers exerted much control and though some wickets did fall, our opponents kept a firm grip on the run-rate. Team-mates made suggestions about bowling

changes, as planes roared overhead, but we didn't
have as many options as I'd have liked and few were
tempting. One, an occasional spinner with occasional
yips, had already lost us a game earlier in the tour, with
a devastatingly expensive over. Another had looked
OK in the nets but had not bowled in anger for over a
decade. A third was sulking on the boundary, wishing he
were back in Wiltshire. The most insistent was the tour's
best batsman, Joe. We needed to take the pace off the
ball. This wasn't the first time he felt that this situation
required his unique set of skills.

Really good cricketers are different from the rest of
us. They know that they can win games and they want
to do so again. Most of us quail if chasing 300. Joe sees
it as an opportunity to get that first double-century. In
that respect he is a captain's dream. You do have to heed
the principles of the game, however. Bowlers often think
they can do the batsmen's job and vice versa. Sometimes
introducing a part-time spinner can work. It can
provoke a batsman into throwing away his wicket. This
is what Joe was hoping for that night in Mumbai. But
usually it involves giving away runs to the opposition.
On the few occasions I'd given him a bowl before, he'd
bought us the occasional wicket, as the batsman slogged
him straight into the hands of cow corner. But he was

also prone to bowling the odd wide and on that damp night we couldn't afford any extras and had few fielders who were going to hold on to steepling catches in the deep, especially with a slippery ball. Straight and fastish was my only strategy.

A couple of years on, I still don't know how it was that he came on to bowl. It certainly wasn't my idea. It may not have been entirely his either. But suddenly he had the ball and was setting his field. The opposition needed 24 off three overs. I dropped back to long-off, mute with fury, aimed as much at myself for this paralysis as it was at him. There are moments in cricket when the wheels start to come off – your bowlers struggle to hit the right length, the batsmen find the boundary again and again, and your fielders misjudge the few chances that come their way. When this happens everyone looks around, wondering how to save this situation. Cricket is a game of momentum and, when that is lost, it is hard to reverse. That is when you need a tactical masterstroke or for your best cricketer to step up. Brearley had Botham to rely on in these situations, we had Joe and me. I was having a meltdown and Joe was about to bowl part-time offies against high-class players of spin. He marked out his run-up and then came in, with a strange dragging gait, as if he were a penalty-taker waiting for the goalkeeper to commit himself. The batsman committed himself. In that one over he hit enough boundaries to end the game there and then. I trudged off the field, knowing I'd blown our best chance of winning a game in India. (Our record stands: played eight, lost eight.) That game more than any other made me wonder why anyone would choose to be captain. Nothing exposes you more than a situation like that where you find yourself at a complete loss.

In age-group cricket it is usually the most talented players who are asked to captain. Rightly so. In another team Joe would be skipper. Everyone has to learn the ropes and that's easiest to do if they're the best in the side. They can atone for any mistakes they might make with runs and wickets. At that age the strongest players can open the bowling and the batting. Once they've captained for a season or two, leadership will come naturally to them. Until then, the adults will often make the harder decisions, namely who to omit, what to do after the toss and with the rest of the batting order. Twenty or 30 years on, the situation has been inverted. The best players still want to be on-field captain but without the accompanying administration. Action is what they crave and they'd like to be at the centre of it. Sitting in a room typing is not how they see their role.

The truth of amateur captaincy is that administration is the largest part of your job. Alex Ferguson once said that no sooner had he won a title than he was planning for the next one. It is the same with you, just without the titles, salary or five-star lifestyle. Towards the end of the season you're already thinking ahead. The best-run clubs are organising the following summer's fixtures in September and October. Others will get in touch with you in March or April, when almost all pitches are booked. The easiest games to arrange are those that fall on the same day each year – the second Sunday in August, for example. The hardest are those where you, as a wandering team, wait in line as all those above you in the food chain book their dates.

When planning a season I have to look at the whole squad. We will have some games against strong clubs with sides packed with league cricketers, all younger than us. The idea is that our more competitive players will turn out then. Other fixtures will be against more occasional teams, where the age range is closer to our own. I try to ensure that these gentler games come towards the beginning or end of the season, with the likely heavy defeats happening in the middle. You don't want your squad beginning or finishing the season in a state of despair. It is also harder than you'd think to space out games over four months. One July we found that we had ten days of cricket, at the end of which we were sick of the game.

Planning the fixtures is just one aspect of captaincy, though. The hardest part is ensuring that you have enough players for each one of those games. You are recruiting all year round – the winter is your transfer window, when you introduce new players into the club through nets. Because you can never have enough players. There is no transfer market in amateur cricket but it is not unknown to tap up the opposition's star all-rounder in the pub after the game. There are players you'd love to have and others you'd rather ship out. I get the odd email from cricketers in India hoping I could offer them a professional contract. There are no sports agents for amateurs, unsurprisingly. If you want a new opening bowler, you'll have to find one yourself. Our selection requirements make that even harder. How many novelists can bowl at 75mph? They don't advertise that in the *Times Literary Supplement* classifieds.

Your team-mates may like the idea of being in charge if it means getting to choose when they bat and bowl. It is never a bad idea to remind them every so often of just what the rest of the job entails. The art is to delegate certain jobs every so often to remind the players that they really don't want to be captain. Those who have kindly organised winter nets sensibly decided only to serve one term, overwhelmed by the bureaucracy and financial demands of the role.

In the professional game few players would turn down the captaincy if it were offered to them. The money, the status, the guaranteed place in the team ... In amateur cricket the skipper is chosen in an entirely different way. League clubs have a process that resembles the papal conclave if you can imagine cardinals in a clubhouse. When the white smoke rises, it is not unusual for the first choice to decline the post, quickly followed by the second. They want to play cricket, not allow it to ruin their life. Do you keep going, and keep asking until someone says yes, usually the worst possible candidate? Or do you return to the first two and keep begging until one of them accepts? Captaining a league side is a tough job, harder than mine. League cricket is more predictable than the Sunday game. There, not only do you have your players and opposition to row with but you will also find yourself in conflict with the captains of the teams above and below you, as they try to borrow the linchpin of your side each weekend, or you theirs. You also have the non-playing members of the club to contend with. Rightly, denied power everywhere else, they have created their own fiefdom here.

The most straightforward way to be captain is to set up your own team and appoint yourself president, chairman and treasurer. Those who do this do so for a variety of reasons, usually because, like J. M. Barrie, they are inept players who are denied cricket elsewhere. It goes without saying that such people have no previous experience of leadership. I didn't. Most normal people do not want the hassle of organising a summer of fixtures. Much better to have someone else do it for you. But if you are a sporting catastrophe, you can found your own XI. It's how cricket started after all.

There is one pitfall that the corporate headhunters must try to avoid. They must not, under any circumstances, appoint more than one captain. The cardinal rule in amateur cricket is that you cannot have two leaders in one team. Even having different captains on Saturday and on Sunday is just paving the way for a bitter fight. As anyone who has watched *Highlander* knows, there can be only one. And as always in life, the lower the stakes, the bloodier the battle. The average amateur club only bears this out, with struggles for power more commonly seen in the pugilistic disciplines. Boxing muddles through with a number of rival governing bodies. Over the years, many teams have been set up by would-be Kerry Packers who flounced out of their club, taking as many players as they could. Amateur teams can ill afford to lose squad members, so this is can be terminal. The best way to avoid this is to act alone.

What qualities would they most hope to find in a captain?

Brearley imagined that a major company was hiring a cricket captain and asked what their human resources department might look for. If a committee were constructing a perfect version of the cricket captain, it would probably look something like Alastair Cook. A specially designed android could not do the role better. When speaking he errs on the side of caution, having been media-trained to say nothing that a journalist could possibly turn into controversy. When not playing cricket, he lives an unimpeachable existence out on his farm, away from the fleshpots of London. When he is playing cricket, he is sensational, defending the good balls, clipping away the bad ones and making the game look so easy. His team-mates seem to follow his lead unquestioningly and with the utmost respect. He is famous for barely sweating at all. Nothing seems to ruffle him.

A more enterprising company might look beyond the safe hands of a Cook or an Andrew Strauss. As opening batsmen, both instinctively take a dim view of risk and their teams played accordingly. The great captains in history knew when to roll the dice and the headhunters might favour a swashbuckling player like Viv Richards, Imran Khan or Brendon McCullum, who led with the verve and aggression with which they played. But for all their successes, there are countless examples of similar appointments that didn't work – from Ian Botham to Kevin Pietersen and Andrew Flintoff. And that's just the England team. Sometimes being the best and the bravest doesn't inspire those beneath you.

Perhaps the key quality is a cool head. Misbah-ul-Haq is another professorial type in the Brearley mould, and has an MBA from the Lahore University of Management and Technology. He has usually had to steady innings, as others played shots around him and perished but he answered the detractors who nicknamed him "Tuktuk" for his slow scoring rate by equalling Viv Richards's record for the fastest Test hundred at the age of 40. Brendon McCullum would break this record a year later in his final Test innings. That cool head can be harder to maintain in the amateur game, when you're out there opening the batting because others haven't turned up yet. You know you can't be out until they arrive. I did make my highest ever score of 98 in this situation, forced to play circumspectly for the first half-hour by the absence of others.

Leading by example is one thing but what a captain really needs is the ability to get the team playing in a certain way. The right way. This is a real challenge. Cricket has an unfortunate appeal for life's nit-pickers, for those looking to find fault in others. The game's Laws offer unparalleled opportunity for this. We all know that the umpires are always right, that we don't walk onto the field before them, that we return the ball to them at the fall of a wicket, to ask them if we can leave the field of play, and if we can return. But it is hard to adhere to these strictures every time and it only takes one person on the field to blow an infraction up into something it isn't. Every team has its combustible elements and they will invariably seek each other out.

The ideal captain will need a hardness in these situations. You need to keep your most unruly players in line, if you want your opponents to do the same. One of the world's oldest ball games, ōllamaliztli, had versions played in Central America by the Mayans and Aztecs. The sport had a strong ritual aspect and the showpiece matches sometimes involved the sacrifice of players. This option is regrettably not there for the amateur cricket captain. Banishment is the harshest penalty you can offer. In football, this exile is often used as a technique. Managers like José Mourinho and Pep Guardiola arrive at a club and target one high-profile player, who is made to train separately, as an example for others not to cross them. But the amateur captain doesn't have the luxury of an extended squad, ready to sprint onto the field of play, week in week out. So banishment is reserved only for the most severe cases. Until then you just have to muddle through.

Is there in any sense a blueprint for the man?

We have established that the would-be captain should be one person, with good administrative skills. But what else is needed? The first requirement is time. Cricket is the most time-consuming of games and many find the demands of family and work don't allow them to spend eight or 16 hours on the pitch at the weekend. And if cricket takes a long time to play, it takes even more time to organise. The amateur captains I have faced tend not to be running FTSE 100 companies off the field. They're not running anything in fact. They're holding down a job, maybe a marriage, and drowning in a sea of cricket-related admin. Fixtures to be arranged, pitches to be booked and players to be herded into the right place at the right time.

The second thing the amateur captain must have is a driving licence and car. The great Victorians who built the railway system that criss-crosses the countryside were clearly not cricketers, because it is almost impossible to get to most grounds by train. The only reason I have a car is so that I can get to cricket. Each game I need to bring my own kit, spare kit for the idiots who left theirs behind, match balls, a scorebook and possibly tea, as well as two or three team-mates. I sometimes have sets of stumps in my car, too – it's not unknown to find the pavilion locked, the key missing and stumps and bails inside. And in the event of rain it has been known for three or four cars to act as a makeshift set of covers, carefully driven on to the pitch, with the wheels on either side of the danger zone. You will also have to arrange lifts for the rest of the side, which is more complicated than you'd think. Not all of you live near each other and there's always one player who drives so badly no one will risk their life with him at the wheel.

Lastly, the captain must harness the power of modern technology, in the form of a smartphone. It's not impossible that one day a manufacturer will produce a model with apps for ball tracking, detecting thin edges and other assistance for the umpire. Until then, phones are essential for locating the ground, the players who've got lost and providing a detailed weather forecast. The downside is that players can get hold of you at any stage to pull out of the next game. I try not to answer mine on a Friday night. And sometimes fielders take them onto the pitch, for those dreary middle overs. Nowadays amateur teams post their scores on social media, with photos to arouse jealousy in those who pulled out at late notice.

Does his age matter?

Amateur cricketers can be sensitive about their age. Some of us who play cricket regularly like to think we're improving and that delusion becomes harder to maintain after a certain point in life. The professional game does offer hope, though. For every player who declines as they approach 40, another reaches new heights. As I write, Misbah-ul-Haq is dominating the England attack in English conditions. Furthermore, at the age of 42 he has a career average of over 48. But it is not just the batsmen who are rolling back the years. On the same day, Rangana Herath became the oldest player to take a Test hat-trick, just four years younger, with a part-time job in a bank.

The rest of us can only dream of an average that exceeds our age or waistline. A team of writers is never going to be youthful, in that publication usually happens later in life. So we have rarely played a side older than us. I am often the youngest player in the side, aged 39. But our kind of cricket attracts the more senior player. Talented youngsters understandably prefer the challenge of Saturday league cricket. They haven't yet given up on dreams of playing at a higher level. Moderate cricketers often abandon the game in their twenties, as life throws up challenges and attractions off the pitch. We return ten years later, disappointed and exhausted by the lost decade, to find that our bodies no longer have the suppleness that cricket requires. The Sunday game is perfectly suited to these types.

The captain's age is important in that it is hard to balance the responsibilities of family life and the demands of a cricket team. As players get married and have children, they become increasingly unavailable, until those children are of cricket-playing age themselves and can do most of the fielding for you. The captain's age matters less on the pitch. You just need to make sure you play sides of the same vintage. If you aren't the most limber of players, then you take your position at first slip and stay there for the rest of your career, even when the bowling does not require any close fielders. There are players for whom this is still too much exertion, however. A team-mate recently complained that he was caught at second slip by a man who was sitting down – the cordon had brought fold-up chairs onto the field. If you are the youngest player, however, you succumb to the pressure to throw yourself around the field in the covers, with scant regard for future matches.

A last word about age. The captain's age will shape the team. Many of the others will be from the same stage of life. In their twenties, the skipper will select friends from university and work; a decade later and the top order may all have children at the same school; another ten years on, and the children will have displaced their parents in the batting order. Earlier this season we played a wonderful game in Suffolk, in which a team long on experience and short on youth overcame the local side. Afterwards we stayed in accommodation that had until recently been a retirement home. As I looked round the breakfast table at the weary, hungover cricketers, I wondered how soon we'd be here again. There could be worse fates but I would have to select that XI very carefully.

How much ability as a player is called for?

When asking this question, Brearley had the Maharaja of Porbandar in mind – perhaps the worst player to turn out in first-class cricket. Once again class was a factor. When India toured England in 1932, it was felt that the side should be led by a prince. The Maharaja of Patiala was the original choice. He had made many of the arrangements for the tour and was a decent, if not exceptional, player. After he succumbed to injury,

Porbandar took on the role. He was not a strong batsman and had the good sense not to select himself most of the time. He played four of the 26 games, and made a top score of two. My team-mate Tom was once mocked for owning more bats (four) than he'd scored runs in an innings that season (three). Porbandar's critics pointed out that his garage housed more Rolls-Royces than he'd made runs on that tour.

The likes of Grace and Bradman captained from the position of best player in the team. Making a century *is* the most straightforward way of inspiring your team to victory but the amateur dressing-room will usually be happier if the heroics are shared around. If we want to watch high-class cricket, we know where to go. We are here to play, not applaud the same team-mate each week. There is nothing more unifying than the unexpected match-winning contribution from one of the lesser players. There are few more joyful things than seeing someone making a century or taking five wickets for the first time. In a game on Warborough Green against the Bodleian Library, one of our players was wondering just why he'd bothered to take a day off work, when he hadn't batted and, halfway through the second innings, hadn't bowled either. Football and hockey were his sports, not cricket. Usually he'd be at a Premiership stadium on a Saturday, dashing off another match report. But he'd turned down work to stand in this field as the game went on around him. Twenty overs later, Jonathan was buying jugs of beer in the pub, talking everyone through every single moment of his five-wicket haul – the dip, the turn, the top-spin – with the zeal of the sportswriter who now has a feat of his own to recount to the world. This wasn't his finest performance, however. That saw him take four wickets, make extraordinarily good sandwiches for tea and then do all the washing-up. In Sunday cricket a true all-rounder does so much more than bat and bowl.

Is he likely to be a batsman or a bowler?

In the professional game it is generally accepted that batsmen make the best captains, with a few fine exceptions. You don't really have to make tactical decisions when batting, but you do when bowling and so it is harder for bowlers to manage. However, in Sunday cricket we still ask what type of player should a captain be. As in the rest of life, most are guided by what we perceive as our own qualities when we make pronouncements like this. We usually want to see a leader in our own image.

Batsmen think captains should bat. God forbid you have a skipper who wins the toss and puts the opposition in. In the same way, if you bowl, you want your skipper to understand your craft. After all, he's setting the field for you. For the first over at least.

The captain should always seek to understand the facets of the game that he doesn't specialise in. My own weaknesses begin with opening the batting and end with setting the field for spin bowlers (taking in much in between). I don't fully understand either métier, as my team-mates can testify. I can grasp the idea of playing oneself in and that the first ten overs with the new ball from the opening bowlers are the most dangerous. But I despair when the rocklike opener stays there, blunting the attack in the 20th over when he should be attacking. Why would anyone play cricket like that? Eventually he perishes and the middle order is left with a huge task if we are to make any sort of total. We don't and return to the pavilion, hoping that batsman might have fled the country in the second half of the innings or used the revolver we left on top of his kitbag. We take the field, having given our spin bowler nothing to defend. I make the situation worse by arguing with him in his first over when he tries to move two fielders on the leg side out of the ring to the boundary. Neither of the fielders in question can catch, and the batsman will easily be able to take two – if not three – to them, since they can't throw either. The bowler looks at me in horror, as I break the cardinal rule of captaincy, in acknowledging players' limitations publicly. I can see him thinking, "If he says that about them, what does he say about me?" I'm much better at setting a field to my own bowling. Then at least I know what I'm trying to do. All too often the captain has one plan and the bowler another.

So who do you choose? Brearley suggested that a slow-bowling all-rounder made the best leader – he named Richie Benaud and Raymond Illingworth as examples of this. Certainly slow bowlers need good captaincy, better than mine. Even Test spinners complain that their skippers don't understand what they're trying to do. Making the spinner captain means no one can be blamed when it all goes wrong. Rightly loved as a commentator, Richie Benaud was just as popular as national captain, leading Australia out of the post-Bradman doldrums. A hard-hitting leg-spinner, he was admired for his tactical brain, willingness to experiment and always adhering to the finer principles of the game. What gives us hope is that neither he nor Illingworth were born leaders.

Illingworth wasn't made captain of a first-class side until he left Yorkshire and moved to Leicestershire, at the age of 36. He turned out to be a brilliant leader, and there were moments when almost every one of his bowling changes seemed to produce results. He was notorious on the county circuit, however, for not bowling himself in unhelpful conditions. He was also fond of being not out at the end of an innings. Both of these qualities are familiar to anyone who's played Sunday cricket.

The problem you face is that almost all of your players see themselves as slow-bowling all-rounders. Even the keeper will fancy turning his arm over from time to time. The exceptions object to the word slow, seeing themselves more in the Ian Botham or Imran Khan mould. As a rule, you are fortunate if the player has mastered one discipline, let alone both. The challenge that you face as skipper is how much to bat and bowl yourself. In *The Art of Coarse Cricket*, Spike Hughes wrote that you should always open the bowling and bat 11. (He also advocates placing the more elderly fielders in front of the bat because they lack the reflexes to get out of the way of the ball.) Most years we play a team where the captain bowls almost unchanged at one end. That is his privilege. But if he fails to get wickets, he gets steadily angrier as the game progresses and I would be wrong if I said this made the day more enjoyable. I would also be wrong if I say that I've never done this myself.

There is a school of thought that says fast bowlers lack the cool detachment necessary to lead effectively on the field. The quick's key qualities are aggression, hostility and a bit more aggression. What is more enraging than having a good-length delivery hit over your head for a one-bounce four? When it happens twice more in an over, the bowler is hardly going to suggest someone else has a go. A true quick will roar in again and try to knock the batsman's head off and onto his stumps. The match situation is forgotten in favour of single combat. Rage is just part of the paceman's arsenal. He will berate fielders for grassing yet another catch, mock the batsman for missing yet another perfect outswinger and once he'd edged one might follow him towards the pavilion with some well-chosen abuse. Jeff Thomson and Dennis Lillee led the Australian attack in this way and were perhaps the most awe-inspiring pair of bowlers ever. If facing them was frightening, captaining them must also have been intimidating. Kim Hughes said "there were some days when Dennis wanted 25 on the field".

Standing at slip or mid-off, batsmen coolly assess those standing at the crease and devise plans to get them out. They will have faced their bowling attack in the nets often enough and should know their strengths and weaknesses, what they can and can't do. And not being caught up in a personal duel with the batsman, they won't allow their tempers to get the better of them. But batsmen are not immune to losing their rag. A batting captain who has been dismissed cheaply is quite capable of staying in a state of fury all afternoon. The times I've opened the batting, I've been run out without facing a ball, having been called for an ill-judged single in the first over. I've been out first ball. I've probably been out second, third and fourth ball, too. In all of those cases I'll have barely given the game another thought for the next 30 minutes, as I fumed on the boundary's edge. It is then that one of your team-mates wanders up to ask where he's batting. The first to do this gets put at 11, always. Depending on the foulness of your mood, you might even send him out to umpire until then. Wiser heads wait until someone has gone first, before asking their position in the order.

Of course, the captain might be a keeper, rather than a batsman or bowler, but most agree that keeping is a challenging enough job without the added burden of captaincy. Like the skipper, you have to be alert the whole time. You have the best seat in the house, able to study the batsmen better than anyone. At the end of the over, the batting pair will wander towards each other and talk their strategy through, as if you can't hear what they're saying. Who better to advise the skipper on what to do next? The best keepers are loud in the field, encouraging fielders and keeping energy levels up. In our level of cricket they have to do so much more, tidying up after the fielders and making their throws look slightly less terrible. Those captains who kept wicket usually gave up the gloves quite quickly. Brendon McCullum, Kumar Sangakkara – even Brearley was a keeper once.

The final category of captain – a non-batting, non-bowling version – is commonly found in the natural habitat of Sunday cricket. It is much easier to keep your players happy if you aren't competing with them for overs or a position in the batting order. Most captains struggle to find a player who genuinely doesn't mind batting at 11. If you are happy there, then you can put the others where you please. They will complain less when you are below them in the order. These captains might be hopeless players in the Barrie mould but quite often they are good, experienced cricketers who play on Saturday and captain on Sundays, to bring through the youngsters and ensure they enjoy their cricket. But this requires a level of dedication that's beyond all the most enthusiastic amateur cricketers.

Taking Stock

The Sunday game is not known as an arena in which players strive to better themselves. The books written about it have mostly gloried in their players' uselessness. J. M. Barrie described his players practising on the train – doing so on the pitch would only encourage the opposition. Marcus Berkmann's *Rain Men* and *Zimmer Men* are two of the best and funniest books written on amateur cricket but victory is a largely alien concept to his side. Yet if the aim in Sunday cricket is to win while involving the whole team, surely it is possible to find failure amusing and yet try not to experience it too often. The key is planning, preparation and practice, the latter being something that amateurs rarely do well, if at all.

What programme does he advocate for the players' pre-season training and practice?

It is a dark and stormy night. Even worse, it's rush hour. I walk to the Tube with my cricket bag and wait on a crowded platform for the next train. Harassed commuters glare at me as I manoeuvre myself and my bag through the crush and into a corner. I get off at the right station and walk to the ground where I get changed, ready for the net session I've been looking forward to all day. Seasonal affective disorder hits the cricketer hard. In September we are taking every opportunity to play cricket that we can, only too aware that we will soon be engulfed in seven months of darkness. Persephone had nothing on the amateur cricketer. The only respite we have from Hades is these nets. We aren't really there to improve, so much as to stay in touch over the winter with the game that we love and with our team-mates.

Not that you'd think it, to listen to the other players there that evening. My group is late, which is not unusual, and I'm in the changing room with a particularly awful lot, none of whom I've seen before. They don't seem to love anything, certainly not cricket. I used to play against a side called the Nihilists, who, disappointingly, didn't play in black nor believe that life was essentially meaningless. These guys do, to hear them talk. Net sessions provide you with a fascinating glimpse into other teams. Each side has its own dynamic, its own shared ethos. We're at the pretentious end of the scale, obviously, as a team of writers. Short of a side of conceptual artists, it doesn't get worse. I often wonder what others make of this team of bespectacled historians, novelists and the odd poet. League sides are brought together by geography, and many Sunday sides are formed by friends after school or university. We are an exception, with our qualification that you need to have been published to play.

Listening to this lot, I question the romantic idea that sport brings people together. These guys really don't seem to like each other. I'm reminded why so many of us stopped playing team sport as soon as we could. The irony is that we returned to it some decades later, when our bodies were on the wane. These cricketers are waxing rather than waning. The most obese among them is complaining about his wife. I feel for her. His belly hangs low, surely removing the need for a box, and a shriek from his team-mate suggests he's urinating in the shower. "Oi, Monkey", they shout – for that is his name. I change even faster than usual and leave the changing room, thankful that I'm extremely unlikely ever to see Monkey on a cricket field. I look at the notice board which tells you which team has booked which net and make a mental note never to arrange a fixture against any of them.

We spend an hour bowling and batting badly. According to the 10,000-Hour Rule, we have a way to go before we can be considered world class. I'm not convinced that another 9,999 hours of practice will do it. Anyway, our net sessions are not really about improving so much as bonding. If there wasn't a pub to go to after nets, I don't know that everyone would turn up. The cricket we play indoors bears no resemblance to the game that faces us at the start of the season, when the cold, uneven bounce and nagging accuracy of the openers will cause our batsmen to wonder why they bother. Amateur cricketers shamelessly imitate the professionals in a variety of ways but the one thing we do avoid is serious practice. We regard it with suspicion and tend to get it wrong. Our favourite players (Viv Richards, David Gower or Ian Botham) rocked up and flayed the bowling attack effortlessly to all parts and so why shouldn't we? Practice was what the players with glasses did. Growing up, no one dreams of being Peter Roebuck, Chris Rogers or David Steele. So the average net session contains little that will actually help anyone improve as a player. Batsmen play their shots freely from the start, refusing to acknowledge a dismissal that doesn't see three stumps splayed. In their imagination, all their uppish shots into the netting race all the way to the boundary. Whereas in reality, they would have been out half a dozen times in ten minutes. April will be a cruel month for them. Meanwhile, bowlers can't settle into a rhythm. Just as they're starting their run-up, a team-mate wanders out to throw down some utter filth. He doesn't bowl usually and nor should he. But he quite fancies trying out that new doosra he's seen in the IPL. Most batsmen are just there for their turn at the crease, after all. Helping others improve is not at the forefront of their mind. An amateur captain wishing to impose a pre-season training programme on his team will find himself sorely disappointed. But perhaps *that* is his own preparation for the season ahead.

How much attention has been given to the state of the nets?

As a wandering side, we are luckier than most in where we can practise over the winter. Instead of shabby nets, where a fierce cut or pull endangers the batsman in the next lane, we have the excellent facilities of the MCC Indoor School at Lord's. This allows us fewer pre-season excuses. But nets are cricket-lite. The sting has been taken out of it. There is no real risk – no first-ball dismissal, no steepling catch at long-off that you will drop, no unending over of wides and no-balls. And on a good, docile surface, you're as successful as your imagination allows you to be. Some players are much, much better at nets than they are when summer comes. They enjoy them more and nerves don't come into play. Some bowl consistently and well in the winter and yet can barely hit the cut strip in the summer, forever sensitive to a bout of the yips. In boxing these fighters would be described as shot. In cricket they play on, as a batsman, keeper or specialist fielder.

There are those who struggle in nets, too. I practised for several winters with a terrible cricketer. He could hold a bat and once made a fifty, I'm told. His bowling was unusually bad, however. He made this almost inevitable by choosing the most difficult discipline, leg-spin. Consciously or unconsciously he modelled his action on that of the South African bowler Paul Adams – described as resembling a frog in a blender. But there was method in Adams's madness: he did take 134 wickets at Test level. Few of my former team-mate's deliveries even reached the batsman, let alone dismissed him. Like Monty Python's "Spanish Inquisition", surprise was his chief weapon. Just occasionally he would produce a good leg-break but more often than not he propelled the ball straight into the side netting. By my calculations, we were spending a tenth of the cost of each session to watch him walk halfway down the net to retrieve his ball. Naturally none of us ever raised this as a problem. If he wanted to master the hardest art in cricket, who were we to stop him? But why were we paying to watch? Plus he made serious practice next to impossible. You need the temperament of a samurai to face a bowler half of whose deliveries are called wide. I captained him a few times and never had the nerve to throw him the ball. Maybe he could have bought me a wicket or two, but I will never know.

In the nets batsmen need to face proper bowling. Ideally, they would bat in pairs, facing six balls from one bowler, then six from another, changing the strike

every so often. The problem is that at our level there is
very little proper bowling. Facing an assortment of part-
timers is no preparation for any kind of cricket. As your
wicketkeeper runs in, you feel none of the apprehension
that will envelop you in the first match. Nor will you be
surprised – you know exactly what is to come in each
case. My team-mates can usually deal with my best balls
comfortably, as I can theirs. There is none of that frisson
you feel facing a complete stranger.

But how do bowlers improve? Not by bowling in the
nets they don't. At least not with batsmen there. There
is no better thing for a bowler than an hour spent in a
net, running in without a batsman to complicate things.
You can chart where each delivery goes and try to repeat
the one that didn't work the first time. If your attempted
slower ball has been drilled over your head, you need
nerve to bowl it again. But on your own you can bowl
that ball again and again, until you've got it right. Even
better to have a coach there to tell you where you're going
wrong and remind you of the basics of bowling. Moeen
Ali improved no end as an off-spinner after being told to
grip his left hip pocket with his right hand in his follow-
through. The best coaching doesn't remodel your action
but makes you aware of its components and the areas
in which improvement is possible. But you have to be

careful in the advice you take. Some of it will worsen your game.

At the age of 38 and a half, I had my first ever bowling session with a coach. Hallam Moseley was a fine fast-medium bowler, who played for Barbados and Somerset. He was highly regarded by Gary Sobers and quickly became a crowd favourite at Taunton, where he was loved for his sunny, uncomplicated nature. These days he is a coach at the MCC Indoor School at Lord's and greets me genially whenever I'm netting there. In our session, Hallam stood there as I ran in for an hour. He quickly identified that my left arm wasn't doing a great deal and nor was my right wrist. My follow-through also left much to be desired. Not only did he quickly spot my technical deficiencies but he also homed in on my secret fear – of being risibly slow. All three of these modifications would give me, if not that yard of pace, certainly a touch more gas. Enough to frighten a child at least. Speed is something that obsesses the amateur cricketer, much more than it does the pro.

Those who watch professional cricket don't always acknowledge the vast chasm between us and them. The batsmen who come on to bowl their dobbers would be faster than anything most of us have faced. Even the keepers can bowl. I remember M. S. Dhoni once removing his pads and bowling some very respectable fast-medium, nearly dismissing Kevin Pietersen lbw. I have been bowled first ball by Dishant Yagnik, the Rajasthan Royals wicketkeeper, as he took a hat-trick against us. Most of our seamers are no faster than an international spinner, often slower, and we don't turn it a yard, nor possess unerring accuracy and endless variety.

The introduction of the speed gun in international cricket has given the crowd something else to enjoy. It does not give the amateur cricketer the same pleasure. Most of us overestimate the speed at which we bowl. The former England seamer Ed Giddins turned out for us when we played the national team of Japan. We'd strategically arranged our game on their first day in England on an uncovered pitch in April. If ever there were conditions that would favour us, these were them. Ed arrived with no kit, just his whites and his cricket boots, having not played for a year. His first over was immaculate, every ball beating the Japanese opener outside off stump. When asked afterwards how fast he was bowling, he knew precisely – 72mph he told us – and he was comfortably the quickest on display.

Practice does have its dangers, however. A former team-mate was unable to resist the temptation of programming an 80mph yorker into the bowling machine he'd installed, "just to see what it was like". The first delivery broke his foot and he has not been seen near a cricket field since. He now runs instead.

Is the dressing-room atmosphere conducive to a sharing of problems or insights, or does each jealously guard his ideas from the rest?

A sport as individualistic as cricket involves a certain amount of conflict within the team and Brearley was not the first or last captain to encounter problems in the dressing-room. There is a hierarchy in everything and it is as pronounced in Sunday cricket as it is in chickens. Someone has to rule the roost and create order beneath them. The concept of a pecking order came from the dissertation published by the Norwegian zoologist Thorlief Schjelderup-Ebbe in 1922. He studied dominance in the hens that he had kept since the age of ten and observed the order in which they fed. This sequence went from the alpha bird all the way down to the weakest. The heavier hens (or those with the largest combs) ate first, while the rest waited their turn. Similar patterns have been observed in other species, from hyenas and wolves to bumblebees. But the chicken is the best comparison for the Sunday cricketer. After all, both walk jerkily around a patch of worn grass, changing direction every so often, and both form similar sized groups – in the wild, chickens live in groups of between ten and 20.

So to maintain a happy flock the captain needs to look carefully at the team hierarchy. Not only must he address the issues that players have with his captaincy, but he must look at those that they have with each other. After all, many people prefer not to punch upwards and usually the person they will most object to is the one who threatens their position in the team. To put it in zoological terms – only chickens of similar size will fight. And fight they will. A group of 11 is neither small enough for players to feel wholly secure as part of a tight unit, nor is it quite large enough to allow tensions to dissipate easily. Within that group there will be a number of strong friendships and, if you are lucky, they will bind the whole team together. If you're not, they will push it apart, as players form factions.

There will never be a situation when every single person in the team likes each other – or even you, the captain. You will find that players' egos can affect everything, from batting order to refusing to kneel in team photos. There's often one sunny character who is first to the bar to buy drinks for his team-mates, and who puts the team foremost in how he plays the game. He is the heart of the side and thinks about his team-mates' game almost as much as he does his own. He might even suggest some useful improvements. At the very least they'll be well meant. For the rest of us, all too often what we intend as advice comes out as criticism. We implore the bowler who oversteps or bowls wide just to get it right, being unable to spot the technical flaw that has caused the ball to come out as it did. And then there are the rivalries that emerge.

So, the steady opening batsman will draw attention to the excessive caution shown by the newcomer at the top of the order – after all, there's only room for one to play the anchoring role. As opener, he's been patting unthreatening balls back to the bowler for years, oblivious to the run-rate, while the other batsmen – trying to compensate for his runlessness – come, swipe and go. The anchor has caused the dismissal of his own top order countless times, putting pressure on them to score right from the start, rather than play themselves in. He says he's blunting the attack and seeing off the new ball. But at drinks he's still there, dragging the team down with him. He's been batting like this for years. This fragile ecosystem is threatened by the arrival of another like him. Two anchors will bring the innings to a halt. I've seen too many games lost with a pair of defensive batsmen crouching at the crease, like ageing gunslingers waiting for the other to draw.

Likewise, the erratic spinner who occasionally buys a wicket with his lobs will not look kindly on the arrival of another slow bowler with an economy rate of eight an over. The incumbent gets to bowl because others have kept things sufficiently tight and the captain can afford to give him a short spell when the pressure's off. But he might not be called upon if there is another like him. Very slow bowlers get wickets because they are so different from the rest of the attack that the batsmen disintegrate mentally. Instead of taking a boundary or two an over off this dreadful bowler, they seek to hit him out of the park every time. Maybe even make him never play cricket again. This approach will often bring about the batsman's downfall. But it is less likely to work if there are two of these bowlers. Suddenly there is less pressure on the batsmen. They don't feel the need to cash in so heavily. Even if one of the lobbers comes off, there is still the other to be scored from. Bowling in tandem, these bowlers can lose you the game in just a few overs.

Moving up the pecking order, there are the larger chickens, in the form of the wicketkeepers. Again, they have a central role but there can only be one of them in the team. Keeping is the hardest role in the game and my experience is that the keepers in your squad stick together. Like goalkeepers in football, they are criticised enough by others to form a bond with their fellow glovemen. And like the drummer in *Spinal Tap*, few of them seem to last in the role.

More temperamental are the all-rounders. These are usually stronger players, who perform well with both bat and ball, and expect to do so every game. Having one all-rounder is great and you can even get away with two. Any more than that can cause tension. Suddenly they aren't as involved as they are used to being. One may take issue when another gets to bat or bowl ahead of him – and no captain likes to give in to demands of this kind.

In cricket players are reminded constantly of their place in the hierarchy. A bowler who has not been tossed the ball by the halfway mark of the innings can be pretty sure that his captain does not rate him highly. He would much rather be bowling first-change but so would the better bowlers. The ball is hard, the shine is still there and the match is in the balance. By the time the third- or fourth-change bowler is on, the game is usually safe or lost. He is either bowling at a batsman nearing his century, or a tailender, hoping for his first run of the season. There is no chance for him to spin his team to victory. Down in the lower order, things are no better. The non-bowlers wonder if there weren't better ways of spending the afternoon and there is as much competition as in the top five.

Captains rarely put as much thought into who bats at nine, ten and 11, but it matters a good deal to them. Our tail usually ends with Tom, who has been coached by Alastair Cook, has hit a six, and yet once finished the season with an average of 0.5. Also lurking down there is our most experienced wicketkeeper. Andrew is nearing 70 and strides to the wicket looking like he's wearing both teams' whites, so heavily padded is he. Lastly, there is Jonathan, whose technique, after years of playing hockey, looks more suited to the days when bowlers rolled the ball along the ground at the wicket. All of them would like to bat higher and I would move them up if only I had others to take their place. Somehow you need to make them think their situation is just temporary. You hope it is but the truth is they'll be batting at nine, ten and 11 next week, too.

Many cricketers are excellent team-mates while the match is going on but once it's over they lapse back into petty feuds. End-of-season awards provide plenty of opportunity for this. Winning player of the year puts a target on your back. Brearley's gift as captain was somehow to make each player feel that his position in the hierarchy was both secure and higher than it looked. With that, his team had no need to peck at each other any more than necessary. The competition between his bowlers he turned to his advantage. Competition in the amateur game is an uglier sight. We try to find that last ounce of performance but the result is as likely to be a beamer or wild slog as the perfect yorker or straight six we'd hoped for.

You have a private income, don't you?

Despite its claims to be the world's second biggest sport, cricket has a terrible complex when it comes to money. In England it is dwarfed by the financial circus that the Premier League has become. Football has the best of both worlds – access to Sky's deep pockets and mass participation at grassroots level. No one has ever suggested that the relative absence of football on terrestrial television has hurt the game. In cricket the

ECB took Rupert Murdoch's money and ploughed it into the national team, with the result that for the first time in a generation England fans had something to cheer about. But what good is it to have a world-beating side when so few can watch them? Meanwhile, the ECB looks covetously over to the subcontinent, where cricket rules supreme, money flows into the BCCI's coffers and where T20 is fast becoming the game's dominant format.

The then ECB chairman Giles Clarke clearly hadn't read Balzac, who implied in *Le Père Goriot* that behind every great fortune lay a great crime. When Allen Stanford, a man whose own moustache begged you not to trust him, came calling, the ECB greeted him like the second coming. The nadir of this fleeting relationship was the Stanford Super Series – five matches in Antigua with $20 million at stake. In the final T20, in June 2008, the winning team receiving $1 million each, the rest being split among the management, squad players and the England and West Indies cricket boards. Stanford was photographed with the teams, dandled a few of the players' wives on his knee and grinned with the madness of a man who knows nothing lasts. Eight months later he was charged by the US Securities and Exchange Commission with "massive ongoing fraud" and is now in prison, serving a 110-year sentence.

Further down the cricket ladder, clubs rely on benefactors to support them on the field. There is a long tradition of professionals turning out for league sides and some of the greatest names in cricket have done so. They don't come cheap. S. F. Barnes, perhaps the best England bowler ever, shunned county cricket for most of his career. He preferred to play in the Lancashire and Bradford leagues, where he could earn more. Today professionals and amateurs still play together, in a role reversal from earlier times. A dressing-room in which some players are paying and others being paid cannot ever be a truly happy place.

In Sunday cricket benefactors are rarely seen. Sadly the nearest thing to one is usually you. One of the unfortunate side effects of captaincy is that not only does it take up your time and energy but it also can drain your wallet. Unless your day job is a debt collector, you will struggle to get your players to pay every match fee promptly. At least one player will have forgotten his wallet and mutters that he will get you the money during the week. Though once a player did so on the way home from post-match drinks, adding an extra nought to the transfer.

If you play cricket with people week in, week out, you quickly learn a lot about them. It is the sport that throws you together for longest. Usually this is a source of joy but some things will grate. This captain's top three gripes are pulling out of matches, timekeeping and money. All three will cause you personally a great deal of trouble but the financial one can affect other relationships in the team. Every team has a player or two who is last to the bar to buy drinks for others – even the professional game is afflicted by this. In the same way, if you're lucky you will have a few who make up for this shortfall. We have Tony who invariably opens the innings after the game or net session, buying the first round for team-mates who will not always return the favour. For that, he is forgiven that little bit faster for any lapses in the field.

Some sports are more expensive to play than others. In cricket you don't need a fleet of polo ponies, ferried around the world in a special plane. Nor do you need ski lifts to haul you to the top of the slopes, with snow machines for the wrong weather. Nor an immaculately manicured and watered golf course. But our sport isn't as cheap as we'd like it to be. Grounds require a great deal of upkeep. We've all played on pitches where the gentlest delivery can rear up and hit you in the face, where the outfield is arguably as dangerous and where the slip cordon is marked out by a pattern of faecal matter from a dog with no love of the game. To improve on this requires money.

In London, cricket is, like everything else, that bit more expensive. The average player is usually happy to cough up a tenner for a game. That is meant to cover pitch hire (for us, anything from £80 to £220, the cost of tea (£5–8 a head), a ball or two (£10–15 each) and, if you're going to be extravagant, the services of an umpire (£25 towards petrol costs). There isn't a lot of wiggle room here. There certainly isn't much left over for additional costs like insurance (needed to book certain pitches) and any website that you might have. Some grounds require payment up front and will not reimburse you if the match is called off because of rain. All of these things you learn as you go along. And all of these things lose you money. You bring in an annual sub to be paid at the beginning of the season to cover these.

Occasionally I long for a return to more patriarchal times, when I could tithe my players, forcing them to contribute a tenth of their income to the club. Jonathan once announced that he was leaving a decent sum of money to the team in his will. None of us has actually seen his last testament but this masterly strategy ensured his place in the side for the rest of the season and that he sometimes gets a bat and a bowl. Every game, he invariably turns up suffering from something we've never heard of – usually the sort of muscle twinge experienced by professional athletes – but will play through the pain. On the rare occasions when he's not already injured, he will hurt himself almost immediately diving for the ball. He then spends the rest of the game telling us about his physical state, as if he's about to die, while the rest of us wonder what we'll do with the proceeds.

Ought we to want to win so much?

Under Mike Brearley's captaincy, Middlesex signed Jeff Thomson for the 1981 season, to replace Vintcent van der Bijl. The club already had the West Indian quick Wayne Daniel in their attack and certain members felt that not only would this hold back the development of the younger Middlesex bowlers but also that it showed an excessive desire to win at all costs. (Though, of course, one should never ignore the county member's innate dislike for anything unfamiliar.) Even the first-class game had to face the thorny issue of the newcomer who is that little bit too good.

In amateur cricket, the ringer is a key figure. There are many ways by which you shall know him – he'll walk into the changing room with a huge cricket bag, bristling with bat handles, with the confidence of a minor Greek god, down for the day from Olympus. He will usually play several levels of cricket above yours, with at least a fleeting experience of the first-class game. What a man with so many runs and wickets to his name is doing playing with you is never entirely clear. Usually one of the captains will have some personal connection to him and has exploited it, to get one over the opposition. Because fielding a ringer is the cardinal sin of Sunday cricket. He has been recruited solely to ensure that his side cannot lose. It is as if a shadowy fixer with four mobile phones has started watching your game from his hotel room.

In league cricket, of course, it is perfectly usual to encounter professionals and quite often both sides will have them. They will do the bulk of the bowling and batting and earn their match fees twice over. In charity matches the appearance of professionals is a frequent occurrence. The greats of yesteryear turn out regularly all round the country, bowling good-naturedly at club batsmen who want to say they've hit Devon Malcolm for four (a streaky edge through the slips, in my case) and then have a bowl at him. Many cricketers have stories of this kind and they provide a mechanism in which former pros mingle with the players whom they inspired. It is part of cricket's greatness that this can happen.

But in a Sunday match their presence is a different matter. I once played a match in the Berkshire country-side against a side that stepped straight from the pages of a P. G. Wodehouse novel. Their XI was drawn from "the oldest and most important of all Conservative clubs". Being old and important is great in Pall Mall but not much use on the cricket field and so they had a whip-round to pay for a pro. They clearly weren't paying him enough, however, since he was not there for the start of their innings. After 15 overs, he pulled up in his Mercedes. I'd seen him before – he was a bowler who'd played for a number of counties, mostly second-team cricket, and he coached from time to time at The Oval.

The wickets fell and the pro came out to bat at number nine. It was immediately apparent from the way he coolly took guard and looked around the field that he was a class apart. This cool also extended to his team-mates. He had probably agreed to play some months ago and, now Sunday had arrived, could think of nowhere he'd rather be less than with these swivel-eyed loons twice his age. As a pro, he knew where all the major grounds are. Finding his way down tiny roads to this pretty but unremarkable club ground in Berkshire was not what he'd signed up for. His first shot was a perfectly timed glance off his legs and he sauntered down to the other end, as we focused on dismissing the other batsman. There are some players you despair of getting out but, having showed us what he could do, the pro then played around a straight one and it was tea. The bowler couldn't believe his luck – had he got out deliberately, not wanting this game to go on any longer than necessary? I faced a few balls from him in our innings and he was almost unplayable – quick, darting the ball off the seam both ways, the last delivery thudding into my pad and sending me back to the pavilion. But he wasn't planning to win the match single-handedly for a club he'd never be allowed to belong to. I wondered what was going through the mind of his captain, who had not got the result or performance he'd wanted from his pro.

I had a similar experience at one of the most scenic pitches in England. A throwback to Regency-style cricket, the owner has been inviting teams to his beautiful house and ground for years, with the unspoken understanding that they lose horribly to his crack team, which will include at least one former international player, and that he will be very attentive to any opposition wives during the tea interval. I still remember my first game there. I hit my first ball confidently into the off side and set out for a run, only to be sent back by my partner. He had correctly identified the fielder as the former pro, who was feared even on the county circuit for his prowess in the covers. I had only taken a few steps down the wicket but that was enough. He dived to his right, threw the ball in to the stumps at my end and I turned to see the keeper taking the bails off and set up back to the pavilion, murder in my heart. The rest of the team fared little better, as we were skittled by the latter-day Maharaja of Porbandar's side. Their captain took almost no part in the game, neither batting nor bowling. At no point did he lift the pressure – the foot stayed on our throat throughout as we were soundly thrashed. The only consolation was that thousands of guineas weren't riding on the result.

We left, swearing never, ever to play there again, and I've met others who tell the same story. Sometimes it was the same England player. Another faced Chris Cairns and Hamish Marshall. Each time the result was the same. We could have returned with our own pro, precipitating an arms race as he then recruited others, but what would be the point? Cricket like that already exists and it's not what we want to play. For once I found myself on the same side as the Middlesex members. This wasn't cricket.

Is there a tendency to complacency?

Looking round the dressing-room recently, I realised something, which was that day I was the only player there who thought he might be getting better at cricket. The rest are just managing a decline. In a better team, this could be read as complacency. In a Sunday side, it's more like recognition and acceptance. Part of this is down to age, but it is mostly due to the fact that many of my team-mates actually were good once. Two of them played at county junior level, two others played good club cricket in their youth and one, somewhat improbably, played for a national side. Not his national side obviously, just somewhere he happened to be living at the time. But he's played cricket for Brazil and I haven't. Yet.

The big question about sport is, why do we play? For the fun of it? To improve? To win? We are all different in what we need to get out of the game. For some it is enough to turn up and enjoy an afternoon with their friends. Any runs and wickets are a bonus. These are the well-balanced types who approach cricket as they do everything else in life. You won't encounter them on the pitch as often as you'd think. They enjoy the rest of their life and don't need to escape from it. Cricket attracts a different type, given to obsession.

Then there are the best players. It's obvious why they play the game. They're good at it. They didn't choose cricket; it chose them. But they usually need to excel to get any satisfaction out of the day. They play to make runs and take wickets. If that takes you to victory then great, but for them cricket isn't really a team sport. It's about them and their performance. You're just there as a backdrop and you come into prominence when you fail, by dropping catches or running them out. In league cricket you are desperate for these players, as you strive to put out as strong a side as you can. In Sunday cricket you want as few of them as possible, even though that deprives you of talent. They are the hardest to manage, since they expect to be involved in almost every aspect of the game. If you are playing a 40-over game, there will be 480 deliveries over the two innings (not including any extras). If you split this up between the team, so each player is equally involved, everyone would hope either to bowl or face 43.6 of them. An all-rounder who opens the bowling could get his full allocation of overs, before settling down to a good, long innings in the top order. He might well find himself involved in over a hundred of them, leaving that bit less for everyone else. With two such players, suddenly the game is very different and others are reduced to the status of specialist fielders, where they will be berated by the stars for not being good enough. The catch-22 is that the good Sunday cricketer will expect high standards from everyone around them, and yet will have his nose put out of joint by anyone who is remotely as good.

Then there are those who have a more complicated relationship with cricket. As we know, the game can drag from time to time. The captain isn't allowed to be bored after 15 overs in the field but a decent proportion of his fielders will be. And some matches are more fun than others. All of us have the occasional day when we hate the sport. Some have more days like that than good ones. Much of the time, they're not enjoying playing at all. Sometimes they're positively miserable. The rest of us joke about it, because we don't want to face the truth. It would make us uncomfortable. We're doing this for fun, aren't we? Cricket isn't a zero-sum game like poker. The batsman who makes a hundred will enjoy the afternoon more than the bowler who concedes the same number. But there should be enough runs and wickets to go around.

It is a bit of a mystery why these players are there at all. Somehow cricket has hooked them and they return each week for further punishment. But just when they are most disheartened, the game gives them something to keep them going. Whereas the stronger players look at the season as a whole, the weaker players are content with a couple of achievements a summer – an economical spell of bowling here, a couple of wickets there, a good catch and an unbeaten 14 might be enough to make them want to play another year. You desperately want this to happen since you cannot have 11 principals in a team, all wanting to play a major part with bat and ball. Some are needed to make up the numbers and so you need to ensure that they get what they want from the day.

Alex was one of the first to join the team. He's young, fit and probably our best and keenest fielder, able to cover a huge amount of ground and cut off dozens of runs each game. We are considerably more likely to win with him in the side. Players don't always realise the value they bring to the side and often obsess about their weakest suit. He hasn't always had the success with the bat that he craves, with a single-figure average one season. He is obsessed with mastering this game. He has spent hours on one-to-one coaching at Lord's and has subsequently built his own cricket net in his garden in Kent. Last season he made his first fifty for us and this year he's started to bowl. He recently wrote that when cricket goes well it was "bliss". But much of the time it's agony.

Those who enjoy cricket the least are not necessarily the worst players. The miserable ones are those with no real sense of themselves as cricketers. We all delude ourselves to a certain extent. Most of us like to think we cut a more heroic figure on the pitch than is the case. Those who cling to past – possibly even imaginary – glories will generally be disappointed. Many of the pros never pick up a bat again after they retire. They know they're only going to get worse as they age. Why not take up a pastime at which they could improve? Hence the drift towards the golf course or the poker table. A couple of my team-mates are not so sensible, still chasing youthful dreams. But your game changes over 30 years and cricket is all about knowing your own game. My team-mate Sebastian has been playing longer than most of us and he knows his game inside out. Over the years he's retired a few times and then come back. He still has the eye, footwork and temperament, and is probably the best player of spin in the side, capable of hitting a good slow bowler out of the attack.

In cricket, as in life, most of us tend to fail the same way that we always have. Then the physical decline begins and we find new ways to get out. Those who have long relied on strength over technique will need to rethink. No longer can you muscle the ball over the ring for four. Instead, that strong bottom hand will see you caught there. Without that extra zip in your bowling, the ball is there for the batsman to hit. There is less room for error as youth's vigour deserts you. But what do you do? Most of us struggled to master the correct technique at the outset. Is now really the time to try to change? Is it worth it? Is this the best way to manage the long, inevitable decline? Would it not be better to give up now?

Did he want to continue with his method and remain at his present level? Or was he willing to work on his technique to give himself more of a chance?

How do you improve in middle age? What are you looking to achieve? It's probably too late to become a good player but there are things you can do, particularly if you focus on particular areas of your game. I'd like not to be bowled between bat and pad quite so often, trying to hit the ball back where it came from, nor stumped against spin. I tend to bat down the order and I firmly believe that if you bat at eight, you bat like an eight. If I were opening, I tell myself it would be different. With the ball, I know that a yard more pace is not going to happen at my age, so I am working on the odd variation. One works well enough, the other I save for nets, or when we cannot lose.

Looking around the field, there are improvements I'd like to make to the rest of the team. But it's hard enough to sort out your own game, let alone that of others. But cricket is like that, it has an evangelical side. If you manage to fix something in your own game, you want to do it to others. Starting with the batsman with the brilliant hand-eye coordination who chooses defence over attack. Or the strokeplayer who backs away further and further before being clean bowled. The seamer whose stuttering run-up or roundarm style makes it almost impossible to put two balls in the same place. We've all wanted to say something to these players. I even dream that the three players in the squad who have experienced the yips will one day throw off that nervous affliction and enjoy cricket again.

Two of our squad actually have coaching qualifications but all of us act as though we do. Tony has recently acquired the nickname "Coach", so free is he with his advice. He earned it when a visitor from Australia took six wickets in a match we played on the summer solstice at Avebury. In one of the celebratory huddles, Tony started telling the bowler how he could have knocked the stumps over more effectively. The changing room, like any other, is full of gossip, mischief and a genuine desire to help others with their game. We can talk for hours about the shots that we all get out to, the balls that certain bowlers should never, ever bowl again and the idiosyncrasies that each of us possesses. And yet we go on as we always have. The fielder who takes five steps before throwing the ball in, allowing the batsmen to turn for a second; the man in the deep who is talking to passers-by and doesn't see the skier heading towards him, and the gully who never finds that perfect distance from the bat, where the ball won't squirm under him, nor the batsmen take a single. It's not as if we haven't raised these things. They just keep happening. Too many cricketers rely on having done something in the past. But 10,000 hours of practice in the 1980s counts for little 30 years later. Muscles only have so much memory.

Selection

First, who would captain the side if I were injured before the match? And, second, who would take charge if I were off the field during it?

There will always be people in your team who would do certain aspects of your job better than you would. My vice-captain Nick, with whom I set up the team, knows more about cricket than I ever will, as well as being a much better player. But Nick didn't want to be captain and so I had to ask someone else if they would take over the role from me once the team was up and running. In that first summer Sam made more runs than anyone else and has played more cricket than anyone I know. I spent much of our first two seasons scurrying over to point to get his thoughts. But he had commitments to other teams and was passing through (but we hope he will return again). So I took the role. In our middle order, Jon has a brilliant cricket brain and is calmer, less combustible; Tony is a much nicer person, always aware of whose feelings I've just hurt; Matt more competent and organised. I could go on – my point is that you will never be the best person on the pitch at everything. No one is. You just have to hope that your overall package is sufficient so that no one questions just why it is that you are in charge each week.

I've been on the field for almost every single minute of cricket we've played as a team, with a couple of exceptions. The first was at the Valley of Rocks, which is as spectacular as one might guess from its name. On the north coast of Devon, a pitch has been carved out of the wilderness a mile or so outside Lynton & Lynmouth. The pavilion is built from the same rocks that adorn the peaks around the ground and is the only man-made structure to be seen. A sea breeze blows up the valley, scattering the low-hanging clouds, while goats and sheep graze amongst the bracken above. When the sun shines, you could be forgiven for thinking you were in Avalon. Unsurprisingly, the fixture list is filled with touring teams who will travel for hours for this near-mystical experience. It is easy to drift off into a reverie when fielding, so atmospheric is it. It would be no surprise to learn that a hermit lived nearby. Or that King Arthur lay in a cave above you, waiting for the call to rouse him from his sleep.

Over the years we have suffered from the presence of the former Kent, Middlesex and England batsman Ed Smith in our extended squad. Ed kindly played one game for us in our first season and one in the second, and so some of our opponents assumed he'd be playing for us week in, week out and selected teams with him in mind. That day in the Valley of Rocks, a young Devon batsman was summoned from the Minor Counties Championship to put our ageing attack to the sword. Coming on as first-change, I had just started my first over and things were not going well. The opening bowlers were regretting ever having agreed to play and the fielders weren't far behind. Our brilliant nature writer, Will, fielding at point, dived to stop another boundary. His shoulder dug into the sodden ground, instead of sliding over it, and his collarbone gave way, as it is designed to. Had I been on a hat-trick, I might have had a tricky decision to make. As it was, I didn't. Faced with Devon's finest batsman, I took Will to the local hospital. As we drove off, a team-mate drily asked who was going to captain, now the two public schoolboys had gone. We arrived at the hospital just as the batsman was reaching his century.

Since then I have kept an iron grip on the reins of power, like an ageing despot with degenerate offspring, never missing a match. I once limped uselessly through an entire game, having injured my knee the day before. I was out first ball of the match, then dropped a slip catch off the first ball of the second innings. I had thought it was better to play injured than for the Authors to take the field with ten – but this proved to be vanity on my part. In another game, I played for the opposition since they were two players short and we had two spare. Our perennial number 11 Tom made his top score of 27 not out under a more enlightened regime.

A season ago I experimented with rotating the captaincy. It was fascinating to watch. We don't have a record of the first match this happened, since the captain that day forgot about keeping score. He also turned up so late that the opposition opened up the pavilion and got the ground ready. In another match, we crushed the opposition so brutally that they struggled to a tenth of our score. Their number 11, a fine novelist himself, said afterwards that he'd hoped for empathy from a team of writers. One of our weaker players was captaining that day and proved my theory that the most merciless skippers are those who have never been given any quarter themselves. In a timed match against a very strong opposition, I'd asked one of our better batsmen to captain. Winning the toss, he promptly opted to bat, overlooking that we only had two regular bowlers, an old ball and little chance of taking all ten wickets for victory. He made 96 and it was the closest of the many defeats we've had there. Another player handed back the reins in the latter stages of a last-ball thriller, feeling the pressure from all the other captains in the side. Then there was one game which I don't remember with pride when the stand-in skipper struggled to take me off and give someone else a bowl. Like all minor tyrannies, very little thought is ever given to succession. "Après moi, le déluge."

Who will help him make his decisions on the field?

Cricket is the loneliest of team sports – the batsman out in the middle surrounded by the opposition; the bowler at the start of his run-up, having just been hit for successive boundaries; the fielder who has just dropped a high catch. The captain's role is the worst of all when things go wrong, akin to that of goalkeeper in a penalty shoot-out. In the latter, you have the chance to be a hero at least. The captain rarely is the hero in cricket – the high-fives are for the bowler, rightly, rather than the person who made the change. When your attack is being flogged all around the field or your batsmen are coming back to the pavilion in a procession, your players look expectantly to you, to make that decision that will turn things around. But what do you do? And who will help you?

There are two principal approaches to on-field captaincy, which in political terms can be classed as Right and Left. In the latter, the state/captain is all-important and will micromanage absolutely everything. Nothing should happen without your involvement. Every fielder is given a precise position in which to stand. One is on shining duties at cover and the ball should be returned there as quickly as possible. Woe betide the bowler who suggests an alteration to the field without asking the captain first. We've all heard the pompous cry of "through me please", when he isn't consulted. With this approach the fielders will usually be in too great a state of fear to suggest any tactical or field changes.

The alternative method was defined by Keith Miller, who, on taking the field, just told his fielders to scatter. This is the free market in its most perfect form. Fielders go where the whim takes them. If it's nicer in the shade then one side of the field will be more protected than the other and bowlers must take note and keep the right line. Players will drift towards those they'd like to talk to that afternoon. The ones who like fielding will position themselves accordingly with others hiding at a safe distance behind square. The bowler will scream ineffectively at everyone in the field but they'll all keep doing their own thing. I have occasionally played with the former head of the UK's Libertarian Party and he was very much of this school of thought, fielding where he wanted, fuelled by the ale he'd brought in the place of cricket kit. He arrives in his whites, knowing that they will be spotless after the game and he can wear them home.

Somehow you have to find a third way, with a certain amount of direction in the field, but not so much that the over rate reaches Test match levels.

You will usually be grateful for the help of various players – your keeper, first slip and mid-off and mid-on, all of whom can see what's happening clearer than anyone else. That is where you want to station your better cricket brains, not least because you will cross paths with them more often, at the end of each over. The player whose every suggestion can be discarded should be put out in the deep, where no one can hear him scream.

Do any general principles exist governing sound selection?

In Test cricket the captain hopes for technically sound opening batsmen, one right-handed, one left-, one attacking, one more defensive. After that, a world-class number three, with strokemakers at four and five, before the all-rounder at six, wicketkeeper-batsman at seven, and then four bowlers, who will all trouble the batsmen in different ways. One will offer outright pace and bounce, another mastery of swing and seam with a left-arm mirror image of this at first-change. Then a spin bowler of extraordinary accuracy and dexterity who can bowl "dry" for long spells, and run through batting line-ups in more helpful conditions.

In the amateur game you are more realistic. For starters, your aim is just to get 11 players. Then you need at least three of them to have cleanish driving licences and cars to ferry your players there. After that you can think about cricket ability. Someone will need to keep wicket. You'd like a player who will take at least four out of five catches, concede a handful of byes on a difficult wicket and keep the side alert and tidy in the field. You'd settle for someone with his own keeping kit, meaning you don't have to ask the opposition if you can borrow theirs. For many Sunday sides the keeper is a figure of fun, and more than one have nicknamed theirs the Human Sieve. The keeper is also burdened with the role of sledger in chief. Often it feels as if the opposition has chosen their most annoying player and positioned him closest to the batsman to disconcert him.

Once you have allocated the gloves, you will look for two opening bowlers who will send the ball thudding into them again and again, testing the batsmen just outside off stump. Your opening attack will set the tone for the game. There are few things worse than an innings that begins with a plethora of wides and no-balls. If cricket is a religion, this is sacrilege, heresy and blasphemy all rolled into one. Even the batsmen would prefer a bit of consistency instead of being dismissed by the only good ball of the over. If you're playing limited-overs cricket, you will need a first- and second-change, both of whom should not be completely hopeless if you are to make a game of it. The third-change, however, can be a terrible player. This is when you deploy your lob bowler, who'll go for eight an over but might just get you a wicket or two. Ideally you want a reserve option – one of your batsmen who can also bowl – to take over when the situation demands it.

With five slots remaining, you can address the batting. Most batsmen will want a berth in the middle order. They all want to feast on the change bowling, with the true dross to come once they've got their eye in. But really they're there because they don't bowl. Your choice of openers is key. If you have two good batsmen comfortable in the role, then great. This is rare. It is more likely that you'll choose the most disposable batsmen to go up top. They are happy there because it's the one place where no one will complain about their scoring rate, for at least eight overs. You are happy because they won't be clogging up the middle order and losing you the game. Plus, if you're lucky, they'll be out in the sixth over, having taken a bit of shine and hardness off the ball and protected your best batsmen from their best bowlers.

Of your five batsmen you would hope that three of them have some shots in their locker and are capable of upping the run-rate. Of your bowlers and keeper, you'd hope that three of them have some ability with the bat. My team-mate Richard, a fine and obdurate opening batsman, was captaining once and asked a player where he batted. "Eleven" came the response. Richard persisted, wanting to know: "Are you a hitting eleven or a blocking eleven?"

The last selection point is about quality. Not all of your fixtures will be against sides of the same standard. Saturday teams don't struggle with this – their firsts play other first teams and the league structure pits everyone against reasonably well-matched sides. As a Sunday captain, however, you somehow have to steer certain players towards certain games without insulting them. The truth is that they will not hold up well against 75mph bowling nor batsmen who will hit them out of the attack in one over. You may even find that your better players do the opposite, making themselves available against the weaker teams. Then it is easier to flatter them into doing something else that day. We would all love to be deselected for being too good. A regular can play against anyone but the part-timers should only be selected for the right games. The most important thing is to have the spine of a side – an opening bat, a middle-order shot-maker, an all-rounder, a keeper and a seamer or two who play week in, week out. With these in place, you can integrate the newcomers around them. They don't have to be devastatingly good, just reliable and able to provide dressing-room harmony.

Is there a structure of youth cricket within the club, through which the senior sides may expect to receive a flow of promising players?

Proper clubs have structures of youth cricket, with Colts sides aplenty. Sunday teams have a small squad and their children, who may one day be enlisted. The players who come to you are promising in that they have told you that they are good. You will need the forensic skills of a criminal barrister as you seek to establish the truth of what they tell you about previous cricket performances. I have played with enough players whose verbal alchemy turns a terrible performance into something passable. They are far from being the exception.

In 2011, Worcestershire released a young batsman, Adrian Shankar. Plenty of players don't make it in first-class cricket but what was strange here was that the county had only signed him a fortnight earlier. Even more unusually they reported him to the police afterwards. Shankar had come to their attention after a run-filled winter in Sri Lanka. Previously he had been under contract at Lancashire and had played for their Second XI, as well as for Bedfordshire in the Minor Counties Championship. His sporting CV mentioned a century for Cambridge University in the Varsity Match, as well as spells in Arsenal's academy and the national junior tennis squad. He went straight into Worcestershire's first team as an opener, and was out third ball for nought. In his next innings he made ten before retiring injured. He didn't play for them again and subsequent investigations showed that he was three years older than he'd claimed and that parts of his story was embellished or made up. He had played in Sri Lanka but not at first-class level, and some of those he said he'd faced in particular matches were demonstrably elsewhere on those days.

Stories like this one are rare in the professional game. Usually the counties check the players' records a little more carefully. But at our level this sort of embellishment is all too frequent and there have been several players I would happily report to the police. Fantasy is a big part of Sunday cricket after all. Most of us delude ourselves a little bit about our abilities and some take it further. I know a number of people who claim to have played junior county or other representative cricket – almost all of them with or against Andrew Flintoff. If their claims are true, the county game would be in a rude state of health and it is no surprise Flintoff's knees gave out on him. A few of them did play at that level, but more often than not their stories don't add up. If they really were that good aged 16, why are they so bad now? Surely some trace of that skill would remain, even as the athleticism vanished. At least the mindset would still be there. Knowing your game is one of the most important parts of cricket after all. Shankar didn't and he is not alone. My suspicion is that many of these players who claim to have played junior county cricket instead turned up to trials there. For these they would have been nominated by their clubs or schools, but there is a big difference between going to a trial and making the cut.

Learning to judge a player whom you've never seen play is a vital skill. In these situations, you're relying on a player's word. Iris Murdoch wrote her first novel, *Under the Net*, about the failure of language. Never will it let you down more than here. "So what do you do?" you'll ask, with the same despair as a hairdresser asking a teenage boy how he'd like his hair cut. You're hoping for a clear response which lets you know exactly what you can expect from this player. Something along the lines of "I open the bowling for my club seconds, medium-pace, outswing. I bat at seven or eight and can score quickly. I am better in the outfield than in the slips and I can still throw to the keeper from the boundary." But you won't get this. Most will claim to be a middle-order batsman. "I bat a bit", they'll say. This could mean anything, from opening for their university to successfully weathering a testing spell from their younger sister in childhood.

My favourite ever response came from a languid latecomer, who'd kindly filled in for us at short notice. He was a bowler, he said. He was tall and reasonably athletic looking. But to counterbalance that he'd turned up 40 minutes late in orange shorts. I put him at number 11 and he duly didn't get a bat. Later, in the field, I asked him exactly what he bowled. "Inside fast", he replied. By this stage, the prospect of victory was fast receding. The opposition's star batsman was well set and making a tricky pitch look easy. The ball had lost its hardness and shine, after countless visits into the distant undergrowth. I couldn't refuse the newcomer a bowl, despite my instincts. But what was inside fast? And how should I set a field to it? As he marked out his run-up, our mid-on asked him again what he bowled. "Just wait and see", came the jaunty response.

The first over of inside fast took a mere seven balls to bowl and cost 12 runs – the burly batsman hitting a four and a six. It could have been so much worse. But the batsman was only getting started and perhaps didn't want to hit this bowler out of the attack. He was experienced enough to know that you can shear a sheep many times but only skin him once. I'd seen enough and took him off. The warning signs were there – the shorts, the lateness, the terminology – but I had to give him a bowl. After all, it's one of the cardinal rules of Sunday cricket that if you turn up, you get to do something. Thankfully the match wasn't in the balance. Just sometimes the terrible bowler will buy you that crucial wicket. More often than not he'll cost you the game.

Nothing changes the course of a match like an over going for 20-odd runs. I learned this from bitter experience and have bowled a few such overs myself. Cricket is all about momentum and as one player implodes, so does everything else, as the amateur captain watches on helplessly.

The Morning
of the Match

Hugh de Selincourt's *The Cricket Match* opens with a young boy waking at quarter to five on a Saturday in a state of high excitement at the prospect of the game ahead. He's not even definitely selected but he leans out of the window to check the weather. It is a glorious day, thankfully. "What a morning! What a morning! What luck!" he exclaims in the breathy way fictional children sometimes speak. The narrative then switches to other members of the team, who make their own preparations for the day's play. The opening bowler is whiting his pads and boots, before a morning's work bricklaying.

The local squire, meanwhile, is having breakfast in bed, while his maid lays out five pairs of trousers for him to consider. The treasurer is also breakfasting in bed, while trying on the club's new caps, which have arrived that morning. The players' mindsets range from pleasant anticipation to rancour at how the club is being run. The captain is dealing with other problems, namely the withdrawal of the wicketkeeper. He has to cycle round the village to find another player who'll take the gloves.

The night before the match is often plagued by worries that the weather gods will ruin the day's pleasure. The professionals may occasionally find rain a relief, allowing them to rest tired bodies. But a cancelled match is the worst possible outcome for the amateur cricketer. You often do wake in the middle of the night, wondering if that was a sudden shower, suffused with the dread that the match will be off. It was bad enough getting out cheaply last weekend but not having another match in which to make amends … That is the worst possible outcome for a cricketer.

Whose call is it to start or delay play?

We play cricket for the highs – the moments of team and individual glory – and grudgingly accept the accompanying lows – golden ducks, dropped catches or one-over spells. But the rained-off match is the worst of the lot. An afternoon of fielding in the deep, without batting or bowling, is preferable to no cricket at all. Many of us look forward to the weekend's game that little bit more than we probably should. From Monday to Saturday we monitor the weather forecast, fearing that rain will ruin our day. And when our worst fears are confirmed, and the game called off, we are floored. It is almost impossible for cricketers to enjoy another activity on a match day, as many of their families know all too well. We mope around the house, cursing the groundsman who made the fateful decision.

The groundsman is cricket's unsung hero. He works all year round in all conditions to maintain the pitch. We only hear about him in the professional game when his pitch is being blamed for a huge financial loss after a Test has finished in two days. In the same way, amateurs pay attention to him when he rings up to say that the ground is waterlogged, will soon be underwater and that crocodiles are ripping apart the sightscreens. The groundsman's language tends towards the biblical and leaves you in no doubt as to whether the game can go ahead. Until then, he couldn't have been further from the players' thoughts. It is usually the home team that makes the call as to whether a game is played or not. If they are courteous, they will speak to the opposition skipper beforehand, to ascertain how desperate their side is for a game – they are the ones travelling, after all. If they are happy to chance it and risk a wasted journey, then so be it. There is nothing more enjoyable than a match when none was expected. I have driven for hours through the rain, receiving increasingly querulous texts from team-mates, only to find clear skies at our destination. Equally, I have called off a game the day before, at the behest of the opposition and the team-mate who was due to buy and make tea, only for the sun to come out and shine all day. Whatever you decide, there will always be someone who objects violently to your decision. Occasionally a player arrives at the ground, having not received any of your messages about the cancellation, to find the sun out and not a crocodile in sight.

What remains to be done by the captain before the first ball is bowled?

The captain's perennial struggle is to get the players to the ground in good time to set everything up. Ask them to turn up too early and they'll do so once and then run on their own clock from then on. I played once for a captain who insisted we arrive 90 minutes before the start. I did and was alone for 70 of them. It takes time to unlock the pavilion, put out the boundary rope or markers, move the sightscreens into position and get the stumps out and upright. And there is nothing more shaming for a home team to arrive and to find that your opposition has done that. It is also an excellent gambit for an away side to do this, just once. It should leave the opposition's captain in a state of furious shame.

The tea needs to be put away, ready for the interval, as we all familiarise ourselves with a new pavilion and its facilities. It is now that you find the showers are not working and that the team that played on the Saturday have blocked every toilet in the building. It is then that you passionately wish you had a plumber in your side. A player with those skills could bat and bowl when he pleased. Then you discover that a fox has crept under the covers and defecated on a length. Park cricketers are used to finding a dog turd at mid-on and mid-off at each end – far enough from the pitch for the dog owners not to feel too guilty about just leaving it there. I have only once ever seen a player remove one from the field of play. Jonathan gallantly ran off to get his copy of the *New Statesman* and used the wrapping to deposit it beyond the boundary.

What can he tell from looking at the strip?

No matter where you're playing, there are some rituals that you must observe. The first of these is that on arrival you must all troop out to inspect the pitch. It could be the worst council ground in London, with craters on either side of the stumps that you could turn an ankle in, tufts of unhealthy looking grass sprouting just where they might cause you to lose your teeth later. It could be an immaculate track, as beautifully manicured as any first-class ground. Or it could even be under covers. You and your team-mates will still congregate next to it and try to predict how it will play.

This is one of the more amusing ways in which we imitate the professional game. Our bowlers are not always capable of hitting the track, let alone exploiting it perfectly. We can't hit a manhole cover with every ball, let alone a sixpence. We tend to begin at two and play until after seven. We are not starting at 11am like the professional game. Nor are we playing for five days on this particular stretch of soil. It is unlikely to change that much in how it plays. And yet tradition dictates that the amateur captain and his team must perform this ritual every time.

What factors enter into the decision to bat or field on winning the toss?

Win the toss and bat – that's the received wisdom. At least if you're good at cricket. But what if you're not? What if your opening batsmen can't hit it off the square and the ones to come are even worse? In those situations maybe it's better to lose the toss. If you call wrongly, there is not a lot you can do. Your team-mates will want you to talk the opposition into letting you bat first. Cardinal Richelieu might have used tears to sway Louis XIII and Rasputin had his methods, but I don't. If I had the powers of mind control I'd probably have ambitions beyond Sunday cricket. And there is no one as intransigent as a captain who wants to bat first on a good wicket.

Your team may give you grief for your bad luck, but that will not compare to the abuse you'll get for poor judgment. We still remember Ricky Ponting's decision to bowl first at Edgbaston in 2005. One of my Saturday team-mates once called his Sunday captain a "f***ing c***" for choosing to bowl first. This player is, needless to say, a batsman and a good one, who delights in putting weak attacks to the sword. After all, no one can make a century against a team who've been bowled out for 93.

On the whole, most captains would prefer to bat first and dictate the game. This gives you time to think and garner information about the pitch and opposition. You are in the driving seat, even if your engine is spluttering and losing power. The truth is that few of your side are going to be in the peak of physical condition and no one bats better tired, so it makes sense to go first. Batting first is the safe option and allows you to take the initiative. No one is going to criticise you for it, for at least half an hour. If, however, the conditions are particularly bowler-friendly – very overcast, with a green or drying wicket – and four of your batsmen are out in the first six overs, they will blame you for not having put the opposition in. The other time to bowl first is against a much stronger team. This ensures that the game won't all be over in an hour and that at least one side enjoyed their afternoon. These conversations between captains are not unlike the exchanges between dogs where one rolls over and submits to the dominant hound. If your opposite number looks like a weak player, you should proceed with care. The cricketer who fails far more than he succeeds may have a streak of viciousness, wanting to win at all costs.

If you are playing a timed game, with a draw a possible result, this allows you to manufacture a close game. This particular brand of cricket can be extremely enjoyable but it can also provide the worst sport of all. There are Sunday sides who shun the excitement of a run chase in favour of an afternoon spent playing for a draw. They will always want to bat second and will kill the game stone dead as a contest with 40-odd overs of dour defence. It is very difficult to get ten wickets in this time, particularly against batsmen who won't consider an attacking shot. My policy is never to play these teams a second time. There are some exceptions to these decision-making patterns. A home team might choose to bat first so that the tail can prepare the lunch or tea. If this repast promised to be particularly good, another side might choose to bat second so they can do full justice to it – wanting to avoid indigestion in the field. An amateur captain cannot always please his players with his decision but he ignores them at his peril.

Batting

So, after the toss, and assuming you're batting first, you must decide the order. The problem that faces the amateur captain is that everyone in your team fancies themselves with the bat. There are few cricketers who don't secretly think they'll come good if given a chance. They just haven't been given the opportunity to show what they can really do. Selective memory ensures that they remember the streaky boundaries over the years – not the rash shots they repeatedly played that let you and their team-mates down in crucial situations. But how do you remind them of this? After all, it is your job to keep their spirits high.

The second problem is that they tend to want to bat in the same place – four or five usually. Perhaps six or seven if they're a weaker player. This should ensure that they can come on and get after the easier bowling. Runs made by an opener are harder won than those taken off the third- or fourth-change bowler, who will serve up one or two boundary balls an over. And once five wickets have fallen in the amateur game it is quite possible that friendly bowling is put on, to make a decent contest of it. Certain batsmen have a habit of being there to cash in at these moments. This is why Sunday averages should be treated with extreme caution. They don't tell you everything about the afternoon.

The third problem is that batsmen at this level often tend to fall into two categories. Those who will swing violently at every ball until they are clean bowled. And those who prefer to bat like a hobbit from *The Lord of the Rings*, preciously guarding their wicket as if the future of Middle Earth depended on it. Not for them the risk of run scoring. Instead they are happy to watch their team-mates perish at the other end, as they hit out desperately. We can only speculate how much they understand of these dismissals, that they in fact caused them. It is kinder to conclude that they are focused solely on their own game. Cricket being a sport given excessively to nostalgia, these batsmen hark back to the days of timeless Tests. For them one-day cricket is an obscenity, but I suspect they would have struggled to score quickly in the era of underarm bowling and terrible pitches.

A captain should have a good idea of his batting line-up before the day of the match. It may be that you have a new player to integrate. As we know, asking a cricketer about their ability is fraught with problems. Unless you've seen them play it is very hard to gauge their level. Whatever you do, don't stick them in the middle order. In the same way, you would not bring them on to bowl at a crucial stage of the game. Opening or lower order is the only place for newcomers, until you've assessed them thoroughly. They cannot be allowed to play themselves in during the vital middle overs. You will know the other players well – if they're in form or not or if their personal circumstances make runs extremely unlikely.

Our opener, Tony – a wonderful man in every other respect – is not the greatest judge of a run. A dedicated husband and father and award-winning children's author, he works extremely hard, often producing several books a year. When he has a deadline nearing he sometimes takes recently legalised brain pills bought online. These make him even more excitable than normal. He calls for runs in a tone of voice that others use in a serious emergency and it is hard for the other batsman to remain unaffected by his panic. I once opened the batting with him and found myself back in the hutch in the first over, without facing a ball. He assures me that if I'd run my bat in I'd have been fine but a captain should know what is happening in his team-mates' lives and assess the risks accordingly.

Cricket commentators remind us constantly that partnerships are key. They are in the amateur game, too. But they're not really partnerships, more short, unhappy flings. You cannot always predict who will end up at the crease together. Sometimes you need to separate people as much as possible. Just as Peter Roebuck's role at Somerset was to prevent Viv Richards and Ian Botham from batting together – they would get involved in a hitting contest and perish quickly – so you want to keep certain batsmen apart. A slow runner who deals predominantly in boundaries makes a terrible partner for a nurdler who relies on the quick single. The strong batsman should not open with someone likely to run him out. I do tend to open with Tony, because even without Modafinil, he is completely fearless – a useful quality when the other batsmen are looking apprehensively at any particularly tall or youthful members of the opposition, for signs of extreme pace – and he has a sound defensive technique. And as he often points out, apart from that one time with me, he's only ever run himself out. But that first season Sam identified him as the most likely method of dismissal and he may well have been right. When someone makes half the team's runs, as Sam did that year, you listen to them.

Brian Lara used to say he gave the first session to the bowler. In Sunday cricket, the first ten overs are crucial. If your openers can blunt the attack during this time, not losing any wickets while making 30–35 runs, you are in a great position. Most seam bowlers at our level are significantly less dangerous with an older ball, and so those early overs need to be weathered. Then your middle order can open up against the first- and second-change bowlers, to take you to a competitive total. But we all disagree on what a competitive total might be. I usually add 20 per cent before saying what I think a par score is. I've seen the openers crawl on beyond the bowling change, unable to change gears. Suddenly 30 for nought off ten overs has become 42 for nought off 15 and the drinks break cannot come soon enough. For you that is. The batsmen may be thirsty but will want to avoid recriminations for as long as possible. They know they're batting badly and that a decent total is almost out of the question now but they won't care to be reminded about it.

Why are most captains so loath to be flexible about the batting order?

Moving your field and making bowling changes are key parts of the captain's job but tinkering with the batting order has always been frowned upon. In Test cricket you might send in a nightwatchman but otherwise the order is sacrosanct. Batsmen are sensitive types, prone to superstition. They have lucky bats and endless rituals to perform if they are to score runs. Sometimes this verges on OCD. Ed Smith, in his professional career, would ask the umpire how many balls to come at the same point in each over. (He'd abandoned the habit by the time he played for us.) In his book *Luck*, he wrote about the South African Neil McKenzie who had to ensure that all dressing-room doors were shut and toilet seats down before walking out to bat. My team-mate Amol always wears odd pads to bat in and he's one of the normal ones.

Batsmen like continuity, ignoring the fact that, if you're not opening, you can come out to bat at any point during the innings. Only the openers know exactly what their job is before they cross the boundary rope. After that the situation changes. On tour recently, I asked a team-mate to bat at four, knowing it was his favourite spot, from which he could play himself in, and build a proper innings. But the openers stayed in, our number three made a fifty and by the time he walked out to the middle the asking rate was nine an over and there was no time to settle. He walked out to bat in a state of great agitation and holed out quickly to a fielder in the deep. I put him in to open the next day, where he fared much better. He got a glimpse of what it is to bat in the lower middle order. Those of us who lurk there usually have to hit from the first ball and perish accordingly. But bowlers can take more risks with the bat, since we know that a dismissal isn't the end of our involvement that afternoon.

In professional cricket T20 has led the way with the idea of a flexible batting order. M. S. Dhoni promoted himself above Yuvraj Singh in the 2011 World Cup final and duly led India to victory. In the current England team, Eoin Morgan, Jos Buttler and Ben Stokes change places depending on what's required and to ensure a right/left-hand combination. The amateurs have been doing this for years. It is perfectly normal to see four players padded up and ready to go in – showing both flexibility and a complete lack of faith in the batsmen above them. If you have a blocker and a hitter at the crease, you have one of each ready and send them in, depending on who's out. No captain likes telling someone that another is going in ahead of him but sometimes you have to add that bit of momentum to an innings. There will be very few batsmen in your line-up who can score at better than a run a ball, and who would relish the challenge of doing so. The demoted player would enjoy his innings more if he came in with the run-rate at manageable levels, or when chances of victory had evaporated, and he can play for his average.

There is one fixture of ours that illustrates perfectly the problems that face the amateur captain when deciding on a batting order. Hambledon is known as the cradle of cricket, where so many of the sport's rules and traditions emerged. The club may not dominate the game any more, and they've moved a few miles to a new ground at Ridge Meadow, but the club embodies what is great about cricket. The Authors play there each year and our first three games all came down to the last ball. Finishes such as these tend to be orchestrated by

the stronger team and no one does it better than Mark
Le-Clercq, the Hambledon skipper. In our first game
we chased down 177 in 40 overs thanks to a superb,
well-paced century from Sam. A year later, we batted
second again and seemed in total control with 60 runs
needed off 15 overs, with nine wickets in hand. Victory
seemed inevitable and I was already worrying that
certain players hadn't had a bat or a bowl. But a couple
of wickets (including an unnecessary run-out) brought
about a terrible period of play, as our numbers four,
five and six set about losing the game. I had thought of
promoting our keeper or opening bowlers, all of whom
could strike the ball hard and far. But I decided to show
faith in our middle order. They defended the bad balls,
played and missed at the good ones and the run-rate
mounted. When Nick finally walked to the wicket, six
was needed from the last ball. In fiction, he might have
stood a chance. In real life he didn't. Nine times out of
ten, a batsman doesn't hit a boundary off the last ball
to win a game. We lost a match that haunts me still.
I'd gone against my instinct to promote the stronger
batsmen and we'd paid for it.

The next year, I drove down after Sam's wedding –
the star batsman of our first year having thoughtlessly
got married in the middle of the cricket season. To make

it worse, he chose to do so in Scotland, the day before we were due to play Hambledon, some 400 miles away. I wasn't deterred and travelled back overnight, only for rain to fall and wash out the game. The following August we found ourselves batting second yet again, chasing a challenging 207 in 40 overs. Our opener Richard made a fine fifty but wickets fell regularly as the Hambledon pro ran through our strengthened middle order. I had asked our wicketkeeper Daniel to bat at ten and was surprised to see him stride out at the fall of the seventh wicket. A good defensive batsman, he was not known for taking risks, in life or on the cricket field. He is a man who showers in sandals, to avoid catching a verruca, and tends to carry hand sanitiser with him at all times. Barring a miracle from Nick at the other end, I thought defeat inevitable. Daniel swiped and mostly missed, scoring six off his first nine balls. With 16 balls left, we required 39 runs. Players drifted into the showers, keen to wash off the feeling of defeat. But Daniel struck a couple of fours, with 12 coming from the over. This left 27 to make off two overs. More booming shots over square leg and midwicket kept us on target. With one over left, we needed 13 runs.

By this time the whole team was watching tensely from the pavilion. Botham might have emptied the bars – Daniel's hitting had dragged his team-mates out of the changing room and us back into this game. It was now that the Hambledon skipper showed us all how Sunday cricket should be played. He took off their pro and, with overs remaining from their openers, decided to roll the dice and bring a new bowler on. This player had made fifty already that day and now had the opportunity to set the seal on their victory. Daniel was on strike and played and missed at the first two deliveries. We now needed 13 in four balls. In the IPL this is a perfectly achievable target but I'd only ever once seen it done at our level. So we were stunned to see our usually circumspect keeper hit the next three balls for four, two and six. With just a single needed, he turned the last ball to the on-side for the winning run. He finished unbeaten with 44 off 25 balls and his innings looked like this – ..4..1.1.4.4.26.243..4261

Daniel probably surprised himself as much as he did us with that astonishing innings and showed that sometimes things just happen irrespective of a captain's decisions. If he'd gone out at ten we would, most likely, have lost. That day he had a moment on the cricket field that few of us ever will, dominating better players and dragging his team to victory single-handedly. It was a truly heroic moment and I like to think it will sustain him into old age. The next game he reverted to type. This time he was playing against the Authors, showcasing that excellent defensive technique, frustrating the bowlers and just maybe a team-mate or two.

There are many things that provoke dissent within a team but scoring rate must rank high among them. It is quite normal to field an amateur side in which the standard of batting is almost uniform from one to 11. No one is significantly better than anyone else and the order is done on other considerations – who bowled, who didn't bat last game, who you are encouraging not to play any more. When everyone wants to bat, there is no pain like that of watching batsmen treat bowling with excessive caution. Equally, when you're out in the middle, facing good bowling in testing conditions, you resent the frustration of your team-mates – particularly that of your captain, who, after all, is a bowler. They don't know what it's like out there, how difficult it is. This is the lot of the top-order batsman, of knowing when to push and when to hang in there.

When someone is bowling badly you can haul them off. There's nothing you can do about a batsman scratching around for runs. If you're really unlucky, the opposition will have cottoned on to your predicament. The captain will have a quick word with his bowler to keep the ball outside off stump and gesture discreetly for his fielders to drop back a little. The last thing anyone wants to do is get this batsman out. Every over he's in takes the game further away from his team. There's probably a reason he's batting where he is – and it won't be a cricketing one. Perhaps he's the club chairman playing his one and only game of the season. No one is going to run him out – he raised the money for the new pavilion after all. Botham famously ran his captain Boycott out against New Zealand in 1978 but the fallout lasted for years.

So how do you handle this situation? Ideally, it will resolve itself – the batsman will become increasingly aware that his slow scoring is costing his side dearly. But when everything is going wrong for a batsman, it isn't that easy to get out either. One approach is to send out new umpires, including the nicest member of your team, the one who finds it hardest to say no to 11 angry men. By the third huge appeal, he will have raised his finger.

But it is not just defensive batsmen who cause the captain problems. A big hitter can be equally problematic, when he has the same lack of understanding of a match situation. He will swipe wildly at everything until he's bowled. Batting for him is all about hitting boundaries – he'll leave singles to lesser men. This attitude is fine until he lets you down in a tight run chase, giving his wicket away when he just needs to work the ball around and not get out. I played for a few years with a player who approached every innings like this. He had been a fiery fast bowler but, as he got older, he slowed down and turned to batting. Going in at the top of the order, he swished angrily at every single ball until he got out. I never saw him play a defensive shot. Not once. Thankfully I never had to captain him.

We have faced entire teams who approach cricket at a similar pace. One side of young Afghans plays at 100mph, bowling fast, hitting sixes and taking astonishing catches. As they get older and play more, they will understand how you can lose to lesser teams who don't blaze away. In our first match against them they needed 24 in four overs, with two wickets remaining. The batsmen went for glory, trying to do this in four shots and failed. Although we won we envied them their style of play and wished we could play with such glorious freedom.

Just occasionally you wish your batsmen wouldn't score quite so quickly. In the last game of one season we were chasing 143, with all the time in the world to get there. It looked like the perfect opportunity for certain batsmen to spend time at the crease, and hit some runs that they'd remember over the winter. But our opener Joe reached his fifty in no time and suddenly it looked as if our middle order wouldn't get a bat. As he ran hard for byes and overthrows I found myself wanting him to hang back, let someone else get these runs. Thankfully the tea interval allowed me to intervene and appeal to his better nature. When play resumed he unfurled a series of high-risk shots until he was out. We clapped him in that little bit harder than usual and the next batsman made his highest score of the season, as Jon, who had already passed 700 runs for the season, gave him the strike whenever possible.

Who's going to get these runs for us, then?

There is an anecdote in *The Art of Captaincy* that makes one think the gap between professional and amateur cricket is not quite as wide as you'd believe. Brearley tells how in a 40-over match against Middlesex, Northampton needed 77 on a very wet pitch. A newcomer to the batting side, puzzled by the dressing-room gloom, asked what the matter was. His team-mates responded: "Who's going to get these runs for us, then?" And Northants duly struggled to make them. This attitude is far more prevalent in Sunday cricket, where few of us walk to the crease in the expectation of staying there long.

There is a stage in an innings when the fielding side knows that someone is going to have to do something remarkable if they are to reach that total. This usually means a century from one of the top order. In first-class cricket you know that your top eight are capable of that. In Sunday cricket, you might take the field without a single batsman with a hundred in your colours. One or two of them may have made centuries in the distant past but you know those days are gone. Hundreds are a sufficient rarity that, when they happen, they are celebrated. Hard, sometimes. One side we play has a tradition that the centurion must drink a "Dirty Boot". This is a leg-shaped glass filled with two and a half pints of beer and spirits. After a hard day in the field, it is surprisingly scant consolation to see your principal tormentor vomiting his guts out on the pitch. Not every player takes up this challenge, however. In a previous game there, their batsman thick-edged a ball to the keeper early on. Even our doziest players went up for the appeal but the umpire was the only one not to hear the distinctive sound that an edge makes. The batsman went on to make a century and win the game.

Over the years more players have made tons against us than for us. For a side mostly in their forties, fond of touring abroad and playing stronger teams, this probably isn't a great surprise. In our first season we tended to do better when we batted second. And we batted second a lot. With a new and inexperienced captain and Sam, who preferred to chase, we usually rolled over and let the opposition have first go. Having not played together a great deal we were weak in the field, and failed to defend totals on the occasions we batted first. In 15 games that season we won six, lost seven and drew two. Five of those victories came when we chased. We relied extensively on Sam, who averaged over fifty that year. He preferred to bat when he knew exactly what was required of him and he was sufficiently match fit that batting after 40 overs in the field didn't tax him unduly.

Not all cricketers operate on the same level of fitness. I remember a timed game which bore out the theory that cricket is a weak-link sport. The opposition had one superb batsman a class above anyone in our side. But they also had two of the worst cricketers I've ever played against. Their chances of victory relied almost entirely on batting second and their star making a century. Their skipper won the toss and, though half his side had yet to arrive, decided to bowl. (He wasn't sending a message to the late-comers, he just didn't want to lose.) We batted well and I declared on 220. My thinking was that their batsman would most likely make a ton but I thought he lacked the fitness to push on much further. There was no way the rest of them would muster 120, so I thought we'd be safe. He duly retired hurt shortly after making his century and the match petered out, with the batting side applauding every defensive prod as the draw came ever closer. This is the risk of the timed game and that is why many prefer not to play them. If both captains work together, then an exciting finish can be reached. If one just wants to avoid defeat at all costs, this is the format for them.

In a timed game, choosing when to declare is key. My team-mate Tim has a theory that a captain should do so a few overs before he wants to. The moment he relaxes when his side is batting the game is gone, as an exciting spectacle at least. If you are to take ten wickets, often with the ball used in the first innings, you need the other team to be going for their shots, not playing for the draw. Marcus Berkmann's Rain Men mostly play this type of cricket and he told me that over the years they have learned not to chase any score in excess of 175. Once your batsmen pass that, there goes any chance of an exciting finish. Instead, you will see an innings much like South Africa's fourth in Delhi in 2015, when they made 143 in 143.1 overs. Two of the world's finest batsmen faced most of these balls. Hashim Amla made 25 off 244 balls and A. B. de Villiers 43 off 297. Had I captained India that day I would have brought on my very worst bowling. There is something about a slow, looping delivery that can cause a temporary derangement of the senses in any batsman. Consciously he knows he must defend; unconsciously he readies himself to swing himself off his feet.

Are we still going for the target?

In your side there will always be a batsman or two who is just longing to shut up shop like the South Africans had to that day. Occasionally a match situation removes all pressure to score runs and batting becomes a carefree experience. We've all had them and they are wonderful, like an extended, elaborate net. Cricket becomes a one-man sport – you're batting for yourself without another thought in your head. Run-rates are just something that the previous batsmen had to worry about. They failed and now you can bat as if you're playing in another game. Those down the order often find themselves in these situations. Either they're playing for the draw or the run-rate has reached unrealistic levels and the only thing left is pride. I still remember fondly an innings of 47* in Sri Lanka, made when the match had gone. Their captain sportingly brought in the field and invited me to hit over the top. For once I was successful and my team-mates were kind enough to give me the strike as I chased a rare fifty abroad. But runs that don't edge you towards victory are not quite the same as those that do.

Should the interests of an individual ever take precedence over the needs of a team?

There are famous cases of a batsman being left stranded in the nineties by his captain, who declared before he could reach his century. Mike Atherton called Graeme Hick in when he was on 98 against Australia, and other skippers have incurred the wrath of their batsmen by not delaying the declaration a little while longer. But what could enrage a captain more than a player putting his own landmark ahead of the team's victory? In Test cricket Hick didn't live up to the heightened expectations that came with his incredible first-class record and he was undoubtedly badly handled by the

England management. He and Mark Ramprakash, two of the most gloriously talented batsmen of their generation, were dropped repeatedly and denied the backroom support that today's generation of cricketers can rely on. Yet they were still light years closer to today's professional support set-up than any amateur team.

An amateur captain will rarely face the dilemma of whether to declare before a player reaches his century. Tons are few and far between and most of us play on in the vain hope that one day we will reach three figures. A telegram from the monarch is more likely, particularly when you usually have no more than 40 overs in which to get those runs. I have only once found myself in this predicament. We were up against a team of journalists, who played once a year together. They had two very good cricketers, a few solid players and a number of novices. This was a game that required careful match management if it was not to be completely one-sided. Competition for places was high, from those who were hoping for a completely one-sided game. I had several players who were going through lean patches and was anxious that they should enjoy this day at least. We batted first in glorious sunshine against a three-pronged attack. One player had pulled a calf muscle the previous week and so was bowling spin. Another pulled up with a shoulder injury after six overs, having dismissed our opener early on. Their other seamer faced a long spell. Our numbers two and three put on 140 runs together before lunch against what was left. I only wanted another 60–80 before declaring and was anxious that our next three batsmen got an innings, since none of them would bowl. So I broached the subject of retirement during the interval.

I met with partial success. One batsman was happy to step aside, the other understandably wanted to get to three figures, having never done so before for the team. He assured me he would hit out and get there very quickly. But as the bowling got worse, so did his batting. His resolve went. He realised what I already had known – that reaching the milestone against this attack was not how he wanted to make that first Authors ton. He eventually fell in the eighties to the keeper, who'd come on for a twirl. The next three batsmen came in and scored freely but I wasn't able to declare as early as I'd hoped, wanting to set a target that appeared within reach – it being so much harder to dismiss batsmen who aren't playing shots. I brought on our occasional spinners, who were much more effective than the faster and more accurate bowlers. There is a type of bowling that triggers something primal in the batsman's subconscious. No matter what the match situation, he thinks "I must hit this", even when he knows that he must stay in. Several batsmen perished this way until the tail restored sanity by blocking the last few overs.

But these situations are rare. Usually the captain is faced with a different dilemma. Should you give someone a bat? Should you let him play at all? You know that this player is unlikely to make ten runs, let alone a hundred. He could stuff up your whole innings at a crucial stage. But he's there and so he gets a go. As Woody Allen once said, 80 per cent of success is showing up. The amateur captain is often sending players out in hope more than expectation.

In a recent match for another team I watched the number seven walk to the crease. He held his bat in one hand right at the bottom of the handle, as if he were already acknowledging his fifty. I muttered to the skipper that I would bet my life this player had never played before. For most of us there is no higher praise to say to someone that they looked like a cricketer. My guess was that this man had kindly accepted an invitation to play the night before. He had to bat at seven if he was to get any sort of a game at all, because his skipper couldn't trust him with the ball. Cleverly, his captain had lent him a Lord's Taverners' shirt, hoping to confuse us for a few overs. What was needed was a short ball followed by a full, straight one. Anything outside off stump could go for four off an edge or lucky hit. Which is what happened. He managed to defend the few balls on his stumps and swished successfully at the wider ones. He put on 20 runs with the other player and in the second innings we fell agonisingly short. His contribution was decisive.

It is never easy knowing how to handle the guest player but you just have to throw them in at the deep end. Courtesy dictates it. What is much trickier is when they want to return, despite their abysmal failure in the first game. In every Sunday team there will be at least one player that the captain does not quite know how to handle. Should you play him as a batsman? Could he be turned into a bowler? Or is he really happy to field and not play much part in the game? He turns up every week, comes to every net session and his enthusiasm is undented by each catch that he drops or duck that he makes. Sometimes you worry about what's going on within.

As captain, you know that not everyone is going to perform well each week and that one or two may even have a miserable afternoon. You hope that at least four will do well, which both makes victory likely and means that the dressing-room won't be too morgue-like afterwards. There are players who struggle week in, week out but you keep giving them the chance because you know you must. The principles of Sunday cricket demand it. You need to coax at least one good performance out of them each season, if they are to be seen again. It could be a great catch or even a solitary boundary in an otherwise undistinguished innings. But you need the right conditions, opposition and luck here.

A weak batsman is unlikely to make runs on a terrible pitch and a poor bowler will suffer even more on a perfect track and outfield. So you need to choose the location carefully. (There are matches that lend themselves particularly to this – in our season, it will be one of the gentler fixtures that bookend our fixture list. In September you are hoping that certain players will do well enough to overcome the season's doubts.) You also have to make sure that they make themselves available for the game against the side of librarians or satirists.

All too often players don't think sensibly about the games for which they will put themselves down. We have a core of stalwarts who play almost every week. I played more than 130 consecutive matches before missing my first one. Nick has played perhaps ten fewer and Jon, Tom and Tony have all been there for three-quarters of them. A number of others play in half our games each season, and then we have the stragglers: the players who will play once or twice a season and yet will somehow take up as much administrative time as those who play every week.

The highlights of my career as captain are almost always the unexpected performances. You ask someone to perform a role each week, whether it be keeping wicket, opening the batting or bowling first-change. Often you don't expect them to succeed at it but you keep asking because they're there and what else can you and they do? There are days when it feels like an exercise in futility when the opener returns to the pavilion, having been out in exactly the same way as he has all season. His cries of pain cut you, too. The truth of captaincy is that you expect different things from everyone. In Test cricket players hope to average 40. You would be very happy with double figures from a number of your batsmen. Anyone who manages 30 is a good player, anyone averaging over 40 has self-esteem issues and should be playing at a higher level.

But just sometimes it all works out. A couple of years ago, Tony walked out to open at Wormsley, the spectacular ground that the late Sir Paul Getty built in the Chilterns. The game was part of a festival uniting cricket and literature and the opposition were a side of actors assembled for the day. Decent players but lacking that week in, week out hardness. The Wormsley pitch and outfield are a batsman's paradise, offering even bounce and value for every shot. Up until that day Tony's highest score had been 99, made as a teenager in Yorkshire league cricket, on a pitch that couldn't have been further from this idyll. Thirty years later, he had lost all hope that he'd ever reach that magic landmark. His family were there and over the years they must have questioned his devotion to cricket, why he had to play the game that sent him home so often in a state of frustration. Or worse. That day everything went his way. His bottom-handed shots in front of the wicket, so often the cause of his downfall, looped over the fielders and raced to the boundary. On the back foot, he was utterly dominant, cutting and pulling. Suddenly he was in the nineties. We couldn't quite believe it. Only Sam and Joe had made hundreds for us. Then it was done. There were tears, celebrations and more. He limped into the pavilion moments later, retiring hurt from yet another of those hamstring strains that affect players who obstinately refuse to stretch and warm up. It was one of our happiest moments as a team.

For this to happen to one of the most popular players – and the one who suffered most visibly when things went wrong – only made it more memorable.

Bowling

There is a scenario that every amateur captain dreads. When it happens, not only do you lose a game there and then, but the repercussions can last for years. This disaster has befallen all of us at some point – and to the unfortunate more than once. The last instance I saw went like this. It is a perfect summer's day in August, a day expressly designed for cricket. The sun is shining down on the fields of wheat that encircle the pitch. I am playing for another Sunday side who have travelled to Somerset for this game. We bat first and set a respectable target, thanks to a fifty from a heavily bespectacled batsman, a former mainstay of the team, who now lives in New York and plays just once a year. The opposition needs 180-odd in 30 overs, which looks to me like a stiff task. Our bowler prepares to send down the first delivery of their innings. I haven't seen him play before – and nor, crucially, had our skipper – but he cuts an athletic, lithe figure in his whites and was an obvious choice to open the bowling. I'm demoted to first-change but can understand why. He has paced out an extraordinarily long run-up and is now holding the new ball, seam upright between long artists' fingers, visualising the batsman's imminent demise. Looking at a bowler you can often tell what they're going to bowl and how well they're going to do it. This guy exudes competence. The batsman is no doubt experiencing that touch of apprehension, as many of us do at the prospect of truly fast bowling. Will, the Authors' wicketkeeper, is also playing and shuffles back a bit further behind the stumps, where first slip joins him.

The bowler begins his approach towards the bowling crease. His run-up is a thing of beauty, his action textbook, and before we know it the ball has thudded into the keeper's gloves. First to react is the umpire who signals a wide. The batsman continues to stand motionless – there is no shot that can be played at a ball that passes four feet above your head. Now the fielders are really paying attention. What will happen next delivery? Surely the ball must have just slipped out of his hand early. The bowler runs in to the crease again, a little faster now, and this time the ball comes out too late, bouncing halfway down the pitch next to the one we are using. Another wide is signalled, on the horizontal axis.

The next ball is the best of the day, fast, pitching on middle and hitting the top of off stump, rendered all the more devastating by the previous two wides. Suddenly the field relaxes. It's OK, everything's back to normal, the first two balls were aberrations. The batsman trudges off, to be replaced by another who takes guard with narrowed eyes. Which version of the bowler will he get? The next three balls are all very fast and very wide again. Our keeper is diving in all directions, brilliantly, but one gets past him and reaches the boundary. At this point, the bowler, somewhat shaken, asks the umpire how many deliveries remain in the over. "Five" is the answer. He seems surprised – we aren't. We know this is just beginning.

Now we're looking expectantly at our captain. In another era, he might have pulled out a hip flask and offered the suffering bowler something restorative. But he has no brandy, no tonic. There's nothing much a leader can do in this situation. A few encouraging words and some gentle handclaps aren't going to help here. Brearley's degree in people isn't going to put this man back together. Genghis Khan would be at a loss. The bowler decides on another approach. He will cut his run-up and bowl leg-spin. Even the 12-year-old on the opposition knows that this won't work. Sure enough, this doesn't stem the stream of wides and full tosses. Having hit several boundaries, the batsmen start to manipulate the balls they can reach for singles just so we can get to the end of this over. Thirty runs have come off it – it could easily have been 40 or 50 – and the momentum is all with the other side. We never get it back.

These are the defeats that stay with you. Our keeper will remember it for the finger he broke, trying to stop one of the faster wides. The captain won't forget his one decision that cost us the game. But the bowler may never play again. No other sport has anything as scarring as the experience he underwent. It's not someone else doing this to you – you are entirely responsible for your own downfall. In tennis you can only double-fault consecutively four times. This is more like taking part in an unending one-man penalty shoot-out in which you miss every single spot kick and fail to save any of the other team's. You're wrestling your demons and losing, very publicly.

In professional cricket they call this getting the yips, when a player's fine motor skills desert them. Suddenly they struggle to complete the most basic motion of their sport, from which they've previously made a living. The Surrey spinner Keith Medlycott and Scottish all-rounder Gavin Hamilton both experienced the yips, and baseball pitchers, golfers and darts players have also struggled with it. At our amateur level it is just another part of the game. Every team has a player or two it's happened to. We currently have three. As a captain I've witnessed it time and time again. You're never quite the same afterwards. No one has yet found a solution to the yips. They continue to plague players at all levels of cricket, and can surface at any time when the pressure is on. There is nothing a captain – however insightful, experienced and brilliant – can do to help.

The first question was, who should open the bowling?

Should you have decided to bowl first, you are faced with other problems. In Sunday cricket you'll be dealing predominantly with three types of bowler – those who know where they're going to put each delivery; those who think they know where they'll put each ball; and those who have absolutely no idea. You will open with the first type and bring the second on as change bowlers. If the match situation allows, you can risk the last for an over or two. You have to set very different fields from each one and handle them in very different ways. The first can set their own field, since they will know better than you what they are trying to achieve. The second will start setting their field, which you will have to rearrange halfway through their second over. The last kind of bowling can be strangely effective – since they're surprising themselves, they will surprise the batsmen. It's how a bad poker player can occasionally beat a good one – if he doesn't know the strength of the hand he holds, then how can you read him?

Hopefully you will have two decent seam bowlers to open the bowling. They might not be Wasim and Waqar but they should complement each other, with one moving the ball in and the other out, at slightly different speeds and with nagging accuracy. You would settle for just the latter, though. The opening bowlers set the tone for the day ahead and there is nothing worse than the sight of one of them spraying the ball around. Pace is not important at this level of cricket. If you've got it, then great. But accuracy and the ability to out-think the batsman are far more useful. The best Sunday bowlers invariably use guile to get their wickets.

Many of us walk out to bat, our nerves jangling. The sight of a tall, fast bowler makes them jangle all the more. Nothing settles these nerves better than a good first shot – it doesn't have to be a boundary, just something off the middle of the bat. Gradually you settle into the innings. The keeper and slip will be waiting for the first sign of weakness to pile in on you. Playing and missing or edging the ball will only encourage them to start sledging you and bring on what Steve Waugh described as mental disintegration. The average Sunday cricketer doesn't need any outside assistance with this. You're capable of mentally disintegrating quite well yourself, thank you. No need for the terrible banter that passes as wit in some cricket. The moment you lose respect for the bowler and his ability to take your wicket you are in trouble. It makes you at least three times as likely to be dismissed.

Bowlers rarely exploit this deliberately. With ball in hand, we crave to be feared, like an Ambrose or Walsh. Physically we are more in the mould of Ian Austin, the generously proportioned Lancashire seamer who ambled up to the crease and surprised the batsman by being much better than his waistline would suggest. We have a number of bowlers who are similarly better than you'd think. When Nick takes the ball, batsmen tend to focus. He looks like a cricketer and they know he'll get them out if they don't play sensibly. When Tom measures out his run-up, he looks more like a drunk motorist asked to walk in a straight line by a policeman than a sportsman. The batsmen are not always respectful. Mark Waugh might have asked, "Mate, what are you doing here?" as he famously did to the surprise England call-up Jimmy Ormond. (It should be remembered that Ormond's two Test wickets were Rahul Dravid and Ricky Ponting, who scored 26,666 runs between them at the highest level. And he silenced Waugh with the memorable comeback that at least he was the best cricketer in his family.) Tom is not the best cricketer in his family but over the years he has beguiled hundreds of batsmen who thought they would hit this bespectacled man out of the park. Sometimes they do, sometimes they don't. Tom often comes on as first-change, after ten or 12 overs. The batsmen heave a sigh of relief as the openers take their sweaters and retire to the outfield. Now they prepare to face the next pair of bowlers, who will surely be worse. The ball will have lost some of its hardness and shine and runs will be easier to come by. Now they can up the rate, and put 200 on the board.

The choice of first- and second-change is key for the captain. Just occasionally, if you suspect the opposition have sent out two blocking openers, you might promote your weaker bowlers and keep your usual openers back for the middle order. When handling the opening bowlers, a captain has one last thing to consider, which is that you will need your best bowlers against their best batsman, particularly early on. Even the greatest cricketers are vulnerable early on and if they are allowed to settle in against some friendly bowling you will suffer later in the innings. The moment the star batsman comes in, you should react accordingly.

The most heinous charge against Kevin Pietersen was that he texted friends in the South African team with tips on how to get Andrew Strauss out. This accusation might have been untrue but in the Sunday game the code of honour is looser. We all know each other's weaknesses and delight in exposing them in the nets. Every year we play against Joe's regular team. He alternates between playing for us and them. Both captains know how dangerous he is once he's set and so we throw everything into trying to get him out early on. Our best bowlers put in a sustained burst, bowling as fast and furiously as they can. Yet knowing that someone is vulnerable to the short ball to the body early on is all very well; you still need the bowler to deliver it. We're mostly too old and too slow. And Joe has seen it all before. These encounters between team-mates usually end in the batsmen's favour. The exception was the year when I found a young tearaway novelist who, on a pudding-like pitch, found the bounce to dismiss him early on.

Is the captain in the best position for deciding when to bowl himself?

Brearley found much to admire in Raymond Illingworth as a captain, and one terrible flaw. He once asked a Leicestershire team-mate how Illingworth managed to keep the respect of the dressing-room when he tended not to bowl when the conditions didn't suit him. Their other off-spinner, Jack Birkenshaw, had far more overs on batsmen-friendly tracks. Bowler-captains will always risk under- or overbowling themselves and it takes a brave team-mate to suggest to you that it's time to take yourself off. I've tended neither to be the best nor the worst in our attack. I usually take the new ball. Then you are matched against the best batsmen and rarely get soft wickets, scything through the opposition's underbelly. You tend to bowl at the hardest times, when you can both earn and forfeit the respect of your team-mates, running in to bowl at a much stronger player.

My worst experience of this was in Sri Lanka. We had an incredible and eventful tour, with eight matches in nine days. But we were short of bowling even when we landed, and that much cricket in such a short space of time took its toll on our squad. In our second game, on a lovely ground outside Galle as egrets stalked around the outfield, I was hit for what is still a club-record 37 runs in an over. I'm still not sure how this happened but cannot blame the yips. My first two balls were full tosses on leg stump, both no-balled by the square-leg umpire and both hit for six over his head. With 14 runs on the board and six deliveries yet to come, it was relatively straightforward for the batsman to beat Sobers's 36 in an over. I cannot even claim that my assailant had played Test cricket. He was a fine player but not of that class.

If that day was a nightmare, another was a dream. We were playing in a charity game at the Honourable Artillery Company's ground in London. Lined up against us were Mark Ramprakash and Devon Malcolm, as well as the former Kent wicketkeeper Steve Marsh and Somerset opener Philip Slocombe. We put out our strongest side, reinforced with the New Zealand bowler (and children's author) Iain O'Brien. It was one of those days when almost everything went right for us. Sam and Joe both hit centuries, the latter hitting Devon Malcolm for six off the last ball of the over then sensibly letting Sam weather the inevitable short balls in the next. We put on a record 290 off 30 overs and sat down for tea not quite able to believe what was happening. We took the field and started well. Taking an early wicket isn't always a good idea if it brings Mark Ramprakash to the crease. He came in at number three and played some beautiful, checked drives that raced to the boundary. He had only retired from first-class cricket the year before and looked in ominously good form, as everything hit the middle of the bat. But from nowhere Nick produced a terrific outswinger which he edged to first slip where it was put down. Suddenly the game came alive.

Another wicket fell and Ramprakash was joined at the crease by a batsman who owed his selection more to his charitable work than his batting. The newcomer looked wobbly and then nicked one to Alex behind the stumps. We all went up but the umpire's finger stayed down. Alex was outraged, pointing out to anyone who'd listen that this was a charity match, but found himself immediately slapped down by one of the greatest batsmen of his generation. In *Four More Weeks: Diary of a Stand-In Captain*, Ramprakash wrote that he understood why Mike Atherton and Alec Stewart stopped playing cricket once they retired from the professional game, because "there's always some muppet who will come up with a comment to spoil your day".

Over the next few overs we got to watch an exhibition of incredible shot-making. Tom came on to bowl and went off after three overs that cost 50 runs. Iain O'Brien kept the batsmen in check at the other end but we were staring at defeat as Ramprakash and Marsh quickly put on a hundred together. I stood at mid-off wondering what on earth I was going to do. It was tempting to ask Alex to take off the gloves and bowl himself. He'd lit the fire and should really step into the flames himself and let them consume him. I had few options and no one looking at me to say that they fancied a go. I reluctantly brought myself back on, as Ramprakash was nearing his hundred.

After his brilliant first-innings century, instead of pushing on Sam had started to take risks, going aerial at every opportunity and was eventually caught in the deep. He surrendered his wicket in the most sporting way – the more astute on the field might have worked this out but the rest celebrated happily. Now one of their batsmen was approaching three figures; what would he do? Ramprakash reached his hundred by hitting me over my head for an astonishing six. I can still remember the shot perfectly, more than any other that day. It was an extraordinary transfer of energy – up until then, he had relied on timing for his boundaries but this was something else, a blur of movement as the ball soared over long-off. We congratulated him and Alex had the good sense to stay quiet.

When you've been hit for a shot like that you don't bowl the same ball again. I didn't want to be hit for successive sixes by anyone, even if they had made 114 first-class hundreds. My next ball was full and well outside off. Surely he couldn't get under that one. He went for the same shot but the ball took the inside edge and clattered onto the stumps. I can still picture the disbelief on my team-mates' faces. Happiness, too. Steve Marsh and Devon Malcolm soon followed and suddenly we had won a game that no one had possibly imagined could end with an Authors' victory. It was an astonishing moment, among the best of my life.

Alex wasn't the only muppet that day. Among the reasons the likes of Boycott never picked up a bat after retirement must be that they couldn't face being dismissed by club players. Club players who go on and on about how they once bowled out a legend of the game. Like I'm doing now. Nick, too, has been known to remind first slip of that dropped catch. In two games against us, Ramprakash averaged over 230. The next year he did not give his wicket away after getting to three figures – he kept going. I once saw him at a PCA dinner where he was about to present an award and he smiled, saying, "everywhere I go, there's someone who's got me out". My encounters with him taught me a few things – firstly that he's a very gracious man, and secondly that a situation like that is never quite as bad as it seems. You are always just one delivery from seeing the back of a particular batsman. Lastly, after reaching a hundred, your batsmen should only push on if the match situation truly demands it. Sam sensibly looked at the opposition, the pitch and match situation and knew to bat on no further.

Are they round? Are they red?

In the international game, home sides are often accused of producing conditions that will favour their own team. At our amateur level, the captain is unlikely to be able to ask the groundsman to prepare a pitch especially for a game. You'd have to pay the local council a lot more than £100 if you want them to produce a raging turner for Sunday's match in the park. You'll be lucky if they've cut the grass in the last fortnight and if the pavilion is actually open. But there is one crucial aspect of the game that you can influence very easily.

Amateur cricketers obsess about the kit they use. They'll spend hundreds of pounds on a bat with a perfect straight grain, pads that can withstand 100mph when the average trundler bowls at just over half that speed and a kitbag big enough for an MI6 agent. What few of them worry about is the ball with which they'll play. That it is round and red is enough. The debate between a Dukes or a Kookaburra they leave for the international game. But you don't need to be Wasim Akram or Jimmy Anderson to realise that a cricket ball costing a fiver from Sports Direct is going to let you down. Any captain worth his salt knows that a good-quality ball is crucial, along with a supply of part-used ones, should another be needed during the match. That day at the HAC we were using Dukes balls that I'd provided.

Everything in a charity game is tilted in the batsman's favour. The crowd wants to see runs, not batsmen sloping back to the pavilion having been dismissed for nought. So the pitch is even and flat, the outfield billiard-table smooth and the balls of the poorest quality money can buy. Their lacquer will crack within the first few overs and gradually flake off after that. The all-important seam is almost nonexistent. The balls won't even be round after a few lusty blows. They might damage the bat but they won't be hitting the stumps. The bowler knows there is no chance of lateral movement.

Swing bowling is one of the great mysteries and joys of cricket. I have played against bowlers in their seventies who can still move it late in the air. Once you have that gift, you never lose it. It's one of the most wonderful sights in cricket, watching a batsman struggle against the moving ball. Remember that perfect inswinger Simon Jones bowled to Michael Clarke at Old Trafford in 2005, having set him first with several balls that moved away? But no one can do anything without a decent ball. Too often a perfectly poised game has been ruined by the loss of a ball, which the batsman has deposited in a neighbouring field. He sensibly decides that it is only a matter of time before he is undone by the movement and so counter-attacks. He's hoping the ball will be lost and have to be replaced – at the very least it will swing less after repeated contact with hard objects. The replacement has been taken from the mouth of the dog belonging to the batting side's captain, where it has been for the last 45 minutes. It doesn't deviate a fraction and the batsmen proceed serenely on their way to victory. To counter this tactic, my bag is stocked with a number of well-aged balls and I even encourage my team-mates to practise in the nets with the old match balls.

Batsmen always point out the fragility of their position – one mistake and their game is over. But it doesn't take much to ruin a bowler's day either. A few drops of rain can fall and suddenly the ball won't swing. A few more drops and it becomes impossible to grip it, let alone impart sufficient revs for an off- or leg-break. No one enjoys cricket in bad weather, the bowler least of all. The Sunday cricketer cannot call upon 90mph yorkers or reverse swing. Without a hint of deviation, he is done. The skipper may not be able to call on Jimmy Anderson, nor to roll up a pitch and take it with him each weekend, but he can pack a selection of good-quality balls. There is no part of the game in which it is better to invest a few pounds more.

Shouldn't we, and he in particular, bowl faster and straighter?

Many bowlers have had a moment like the one Ben Stokes suffered in the 2016 World Cup final. If he could bowl an over that went for fewer than 18 runs, England would be T20 world champions. At the other end was Carlos Brathwaite, a young West Indian all-rounder who had yet to announce himself to the world. When he hit Stokes's first four balls for six he ensured a place for himself in cricket's pantheon. The Englishman experienced what many an amateur has before him, as perfectly decent deliveries disappear to the boundary, sometimes without bouncing, one after another. Try as you might, every ball you bowl meets the middle of the bat and flies over your head for another six. It's not that your brain freezes. Instead your blood has started pumping and you're in fight mode. You want to blast this batsman out, with a significantly quicker delivery that squeezes under his bat and plucks out middle stump. But that just isn't going to happen. After conferring with Brearley, Bob Willis bowled faster and straighter at Headingley in 1981, but few of us can find that extra yard of pace to hurry a class batsman. You're just giving him what he wants – more of the same. Practice.

It is always a shock as a bowler when your first ball is hit for six. Maybe it shouldn't be. It's happened enough. But what do you do next? You'd quite like to go home, but you can't. This is cricket after all and you have to finish your over. Many bowlers begin with their stock length delivery and the temptation is often to repeat it. In poker, they say that if the first bullet doesn't work, fire another. In other words, raise again. The length ball will work this time. It was luck that the batsman read the ball's movement perfectly and swung it high over the rope. But once he's done it a second time, it really is time to rethink. The problem is that he's destroyed your best delivery. What will he do to the other ones? As a decent amateur bowler you hope that your stock ball will come out OK five times out of six. Six if you're bowling well. But you haven't practised your variations anything like as much and so the off- or leg-cutter can easily go wrong. There, you're looking at three or four out of six doing what they're meant to. You have your slower ball, which is far too readable. It hasn't even deceived anyone in the nets, not even your tailenders. And you're not quick enough to try a bouncer, not on this pitch. Maybe it's best to keep it simple. Suddenly you're back where you started, planning to bowl length.

For an international player, it's slightly different, of course. These contests are like an elite game of rock, paper, scissors with both players trying to predict what the other will do and acting accordingly. Yorker, bouncer, slower ball? It's hard to outwit a player who is much, much better than you. You don't have the skill to follow him as he steps to leg, cramping him for room. You'd probably dislocate your shoulder bowling that variation out of the back of your hand. Nor can you be sure that your yorkers won't all be low full tosses. The temptation is to change everything around. There are players who can do it – I've seen my team-mate Andy bowl right- and left-arm both over and round the wicket in a single over, all perfectly respectable deliveries. But no matter how badly it's going, you mustn't switch to spin. That, after all, is what Malcolm Nash was doing that day in Glamorgan when Gary Sobers hit him for six sixes in an over. Up until then he'd been a left-arm seamer but that day he span his way into the history books.

So what can the captain do when his bowler is under assault? By this stage your best fielders should be at cow corner, long-on and long-off. I've set fields with five men on the leg-side boundary. But sometimes it doesn't matter where you put them, since the batsman is clearing them each time. The Sunday cricketer has yet to master the athletic leap we see in the IPL, when they parry the ball down to a team-mate waiting just inside the rope. It's hard enough to get one fielder to run to the boundary, let alone two. All too often, they collide in their attempts to stop the ball and a third fielder has to retrieve the ball and help them to their feet.

What the bowler needs to do is add variety of a different type. Bowling round the wicket, from wider in the crease, or from a yard further back than usual. Or just pray the batsman doesn't quite time one and takes a single. I have been in this situation perhaps more times than anyone else in my team. This is the lot of the second- or third-best bowler in the side. As captain of an amateur team, your strike bowler is too good to suffer this fate and the others you consider – perhaps wrongly – not good enough to throw in against the former professional. Of my most disastrous overs (and I classify anything over 20 as disastrous), only two of them contained wides or no-balls. The rest were all scored off six deliveries. But when you're really outclassed, you have one last option – your very worst bowler. It's time to bring out the gimp.

What happened?

As captain, there are games that stay with you for years and not for the right reasons. The worst tend to be those when there is conflict within your team. But there are others when the conflict is within *you*. You keep asking yourself afterwards if you did the right thing, if you were on the right side even. It was one of those weeks when I had far too much on and yet here I was playing cricket against a team of actors that we face each year. It can complicate things if you like the opposition. You don't want to crush them. Really you want them to enjoy the afternoon, just not quite as much as you do. We batted first and I went out to open – this was one of those days when the order was done by time of arrival. The opposition had a good young left-arm quick, who'd played not too long ago at county junior level. So I put a helmet on. I needed it for his third delivery, a bouncer which hurtled through my attempted pull and onto the metal encasing my head. The next two balls were also short, sending me rocking back in my crease, before the last, full and fast, plucked out my off stump. I could only dream of dismissing a batsman in this way, with this four-card trick.

I walked back to the pavilion, thinking that my afternoon could only improve. The other batsmen all coped better and by tea we had 255 on the board, off 40 overs. Illness and injury had deprived us of two of our more incisive bowlers but I was confident that our attack could defend this imposing total. We had two reliable seamers (Tom and me), a brace of expensive change bowlers (both called Jonathan) and Steve, a visiting Australian who had played grade cricket and who was feeling his way back after a decade out of the game. I opened with Tom and the second Jonathan, a swing bowler whose practice run-up was faster than anything he'd manage the rest of the afternoon. One batsman hit a flurry of boundaries before edging behind. After 20 overs, the actors were 70 for one. They needed 186 off the next 20 overs. I had barely gone for a run and Steve was bowling well at the other end. It was time to loosen the belt a notch or two.

The change bowlers made things happen, as they invariably do. The run-rate shot up appreciably but wickets also fell. Getting players out is not always a good thing in Sunday games, since the left-arm quick was in next. You have to know an opposition very well before deciding to keep batsmen in. It's a very risky strategy and I very rarely do it. The new batsman set about our attack intelligently, never quite hitting anyone out of the attack. A couple of my side cast nervous glances at me. Surely I should be bringing myself back on and squeezing the life out of this game. But with the required run-rate up at ten an over, I thought we were safe. For the time being at least. Then with five overs left and 60 runs needed, I came back for my second spell. But I was bowling at a very different batsman to the previous, more defensive ones. And I was knackered. By cricket, by the demands of my job, by running a team, by a terrible night's sleep, by everything.

Despite all these excuses, I would expect to defend 12 an over at the death against most batsmen. But this was not the time to get the yips. I've had a few yippy moments over the years, usually when my muscles were screaming for me to stop, after 15 overs on the trot. Bowling is a very unnatural action for the human body and it puts incredible stress on it. Even an amateur seam bowler will be managing a number of minor injuries during the season. With me it's shin splints and my right rotator cuff that are first to flare up. Others have more recondite muscles that you're not even sure you possess when they mention their latest strain.

What would usually happen with me is that a couple of stock deliveries would come out wrong and I would know that I was spent and should come off. This time as I ran in everything felt askew. I knew the ball wasn't going to come out right before it left my hand. Having conceded just three runs in my previous five overs, I now went for 28 in nine balls. I bowled a sequence of full tosses and long-hops to a good batsman who was nearing a century. The required rate was not quite halved but after that the chase was a formality. Neither Tom nor Steve could defend 32 in four – nor should they have had to. The exultant actors cheered what must have been one of their more unexpected victories. My team trooped off the field, into the shower, car and then back home. Richard and I accompanied the beaming opposition to the pub. A couple of them were kind enough to acknowledge that I'd "made a game of it". But the truth of it is that we had desperately wanted to win but I'd been undone by the thrill of gambling with the outcome.

A match like this provides endless food for thought. Would I have been more ruthless with a different opposition? Answer – yes. I like this team and have played for them in the past. In fact, I play much better for them than I do against them. Would we have won with the original team selected? Probably, since we would have had four good bowlers with a lot of cricket under their belt this summer. Would we have won if I'd had an earlier night and hadn't played the day before? That I don't know. It's always tempting to reduce cricket and the result to being just about you. This was as clear a case as you get of one person losing the match for his team. I will always be asking is "will this happen to me again?" I have no idea but I do know that the more I think about it, the more likely it is that it shall. There are always other factors in a defeat. It's rarely just about one player. Jonathan is equally convinced that it was all his fault. But I was captain that day, as well as the bowler who went to pieces. It was my plan that I executed so badly.

Should you give your fastest bowler one or at most two overs before the interval?

The most valuable piece of advice I was ever given as a captain went as follows: the moment you ask yourself if you should take a bowler off, you should do it right then. Don't give them another over or two. It'll be too late. Take them off there and then. You can guarantee your team-mates have had the same idea. The batsman is settling more comfortably into his stance. The bowler's threat is diminished. The fielders already look less alert. Really you should be thinking constantly about changing the bowling. What would the batsman least like to face? I remember once watching a T20 match where M. S. Dhoni made 18 bowling changes. No one bowled more than one over in a row. The batsmen weren't able to settle.

Batsmen operate on instinct, spend hours in the nets practising shots and building muscle memory. Making them think can be a good thing and can interfere with their unconscious decision-making. Your bowlers are not the highly tuned athletes that are seen in the IPL, however, and many will struggle with the idea of bowling short spells. They will all talk of rhythm, as if they would bowl the perfect over if you left them on long enough. No bowler likes being taken off and we all say "just one more" to our captain. Sometimes it works, sometimes it doesn't. But he'll resent you if the gambit doesn't work.

Rather than bringing on your best bowler just before the interval, why not throw the ball to the worst? We have all seen excellent batsmen fall to bad bowling, having weathered much more testing stuff. The low full toss, the looping leg-break that doesn't turn – no one practises against these. There is no bowling machine setting for truly awful bowling. This is a surprise weapon in the amateur captain's arsenal, and just sometimes it'll get you that wicket. Once the batsman has gone, the bowler can come off. He's done his job.

I have seen these bowlers like this scythe through an opposition. In one game the purveyor of lobs took five wickets, dismissing a number of competent batsmen. I had invited a friend from India to play at a lovely ground in Somerset. Diggy is a player of considerable class with many fine hundreds to his name. He knew that English conditions were different but not that different. Facing a bowler like that is not something he expected to happen in the 21st century. It was as if a time portal had opened up and this bowler walked out of the Victorian age. Like the rest of us, my friend surrendered his wicket cheaply.

Taking
the Field

It is safe to say that relatively few great leaders of men are lurking in the world of village cricket. They are mostly too busy shouting in the boardroom, or perhaps writing books and teaching classes on leadership. Most of us who captain amateur cricket teams would hesitate to describe ourselves as natural leaders. I have never read *The Art of War* nor can I recite speeches from *Any Given Sunday* or *Henry V*. I've barely given a team talk in my life. Those that I attempted fell embarrassingly flat, as my team-mates looked on sympathetically. If there's a tougher crowd for a speechmaker than a group of writers, I've yet to encounter it. But the skippers will secretly pride themselves on their grasp of strategy and tactics. This manifests itself most in field placings. If you ever want to compliment a skipper, tell him that he positioned his players perfectly. This is the aspect of the game a captain needs to master above all else. It's the area in which you will find yourself most exposed.

What else can a fielding team expect of its leader? And what should he ask of them?

Firstly, you have to start with your own fielding. It's nigh-on impossible to have any authority if you are the worst in the field in the side. Fielding is the part of cricket that few love. When even high-profile international cricketers talk of how much they hated it, what hope does the amateur captain have of rousing his troops in the field? And yet it is the easiest discipline in which you and your team-mates can improve. Bowling and batting require particular physical attributes if you are to excel, whereas a bit of practice can do wonders with catching and ground fielding. (It is harder to bring back those throwing arms from the dead.) But there is a terrible contradiction – while few of your players will show even the slightest inclination to improve their fielding through practice, all will have views on how you can improve your field settings. They believe there is a kind of positional alchemy – a golden mean – that will make up for their deficiencies and cowardice when the ball is coming hard towards them.

There is a huge element of luck in setting a field, particularly at a level of the game where the bowler doesn't always know where he's going to put the ball and the batsman is pleased to find the middle of the bat. You should also factor in the fielder's ability to wander up to 20 yards from where you positioned him over the course of the afternoon. Marcus Berkmann defined this phenomenon perfectly as "stonedrift" – as if some gigantic natural force gathered up this human moraine and left it at deep extra cover. But despite all of this there are some rules that it is wise to follow.

In poker there is a well-known maxim that if you can't spot the sucker at the table within the first hour, it's you. This doesn't apply in cricket. You can have a whole team of duffers in the field. Everyone has a theory about the best place to hide a bad fielder. But that's assuming there's only one. What happens when they outnumber the good fielders? How do you make the most of your sole good fielder? You can't put him at slip as you might in a stronger team. You'll find yourself wanting to move him after every ball to where it's just gone. But every fielder is different and this applies to the weaker ones most of all. Some of your side will be able to run, others catch, and, if you're lucky, a few can do both. Very few will be able to throw. The idea of a team-mate effortlessly hurling the ball, flat and fast, into the keeper's hands is one that the amateur captain should swiftly put out of his mind. Your job is to identify your team's fielding strengths and weaknesses and place them in a position to maximise the former and minimise the latter. Which is harder than it sounds. Lastly, you have to keep them interested somehow for the whole innings. A team-mate used to play for a side that struggled terribly in the field. A couple of the players couldn't face the prospect of a long stint in the field without stimulants and took ecstasy during the tea interval. This became apparent some overs later and they were banished into the deep.

What field should a fast bowler have at the start of an innings?

The first question is where do you start with your field setting? Your opening bowlers are ready. One is marking out his run-up, the other drifting down to third man or fine leg. The keeper is working out how far back he needs to stand. The captain traditionally either stands next to him at first slip or at mid-off. This time what works in the professional game works for you, too. In both positions you can see if the ball is moving and how the batsman is reacting to each delivery. At mid-off you can talk to the bowler and devise some sort of strategy. At slip you get the keeper's input. Both positions involve the ball coming to you at speed. If you don't set an example in stopping the hard-hit ball, don't be surprised if others dive out of the way.

Now you have to position the eight remaining players. Do you place your worst fielder first or your best one? If you always do the same thing, your team will soon work it out. Let us start with the worst fielder. You have several options. The first and traditional one is to put him at mid-on. The on-drive is one of the hardest shots to play well and so the ball is usually not going to be hit as hard as it would be elsewhere in the ring. So if your worst player is reasonably mobile, this isn't a bad option. The most immobile fielder is usually stationed at first slip, because he can't run and he did once take a catch there a decade ago. Some captains like to position their weakest fielder behind the bat, at either third man or fine leg, and so you see this poor man scurrying from one end of the ground to the other at the end of every over. It is kinder if a weaker fielder alternates third man with mid-on at each end. But there is a lot to be said for having someone who can throw down at third man or fine leg. A great many run outs come from shots hit behind square, where the non-striker is supposed to call for the run and a player with a hard, fast throw can capitalise on any confusion. And it gives your bowler a chance to rest.

An alternative is to hide the bad player in plain sight. The Russians have a word, *maskirovka*, to describe the concept of military deception, building armies of dummy tanks and concealing defences to make your enemy think you're strong where you're weak and weak where you're strong. In the same way, you need to convince the batsmen that there is no vulnerability in your fielding circle, that all of your players can catch and throw. Station your worst fielder at short extra cover or silly mid-off, in sunglasses, so the opposition can't see the fear in his eyes. Every over in which they don't work him out is a small triumph.

With the bowler, keeper, slip and fine leg taken care of, it's time to place the other fielders. Looking round the field, you will have cover next to you at mid-off – traditionally where you place your best and youngest fielder. Then point, also a position requiring agility and good hands – though W. G. Grace fielded there, even in his later years. (It is no bad thing to have your most imposing cricketer in the batsman's eyeline.) If you have weak fielders in the covers, you'll need a lot of them. There really is no place to hide and the ball tends to be hit harder through there than anywhere else. Not the cover drive, but the flat-batted cut. Only the quicker bowlers are cut fiercely square of the wicket.

The positions of gully and slip allow you some creativity. Few bowlers at this level have the pace and accuracy to require that you place your best fielders there – though a lively pitch could change that. I would also argue that they are the most overused positions in Sunday cricket. Only the best bowlers should have a slip and even then only for their first spell. But it is quite usual to see first slip stay there all game, as the rest of the field does its best to limit the runs. I remember asking Richard to go to gully in a game on tour in which we were being run ragged. I still remember the tone of scorn in which he said "You want a gully? Now?" He was right, of course. Most of the time in those situations you want one nimble fielder quite close in on each side, and the rest of the field spread to stop boundaries.

The positions of square leg and midwicket can involve turning to fetch the bad ball from the boundary, but both should be alert for the mishit to leg – there is nothing that lifts a team more than a screamer taken from a full-blooded shot.

Lastly, we come to the wicketkeeper, who is the most important player in your team after the captain. Like you, he sets the tone for your team's performance, being involved in every ball. If he is good with the gloves, the whole team will respond accordingly. If you are a quiet captain, he takes on even more importance. He will provide the constant verbal encouragement to the bowlers and fielders that will keep the side going in those stagnant overs when nothing much is happening. He can lift your side with a virtuoso piece of glovemanship. In *The Jubilee Book of Cricket* Prince Ranjitsinhji wrote that, when choosing a keeper, catches were paramount, then stumpings, run outs and finally byes. This is why even at our level you see the keeper standing up to a batsman who has taken guard outside the crease. He wants to attack, though he will probably fail to take most of the balls cleanly. Only our most regular keeper, Will, is able to do this well. He is one of the first names on the team sheet and as good behind the stumps as anyone I've seen at our level. At least once a season a non-keeper has to take the gloves and only then do we see what we're missing.

How attacking should we be?

Let's start with the first over and assume your opening bowler swings the ball away from the right-handed batsman with reasonable accuracy. You might want to move your best fielders from cover and point and put them in the slips. You will want two mobile fielders on the on-side, at wide mid-on and fine leg. They aren't there to take any catches, just tidy up after the mishits to leg and any bad balls. Michael Clarke was known for his funky fields and there is a lot to be said for a short extra cover at an early stage of a game, as the batsman gets accustomed to the pace of the bowler and the pitch. A catch is likely to come just in front of the bat, from a mistimed shot as the batsman gets accustomed to the pace of the pitch – or the opening bowler, whose long run-up gives the lie to the delivery to follow. You can populate the covers with your weaker fielders, hoping that quantity will be a quality. But one of them should be able to throw, there being nothing sadder than the sight of a fielder overhauling the ball near the boundary, unable to propel it further than ten yards.

It's quite possible in these cases for the batsmen to run more than four.

As you move around for the second over, you turn to your other opener, who bowls stump to stump, bringing the ball into the right-hander. Now you might want your best fielders at midwicket and square leg. Your least mobile player can return to first slip, where he's less likely to be exposed than in the previous over. While the ball is swinging you're attacking and you might consider a close catcher on the leg side. This being amateur cricket, it is unlikely that you'll have anyone with the superb reflexes and courage needed at short leg but it's amazing how distracting a presence in the batsman's eyeline can be. Gully is not so important now and you might even take out cover, to encourage the batsman to drive and be bowled through the gate.

During these overs you'll be fine-tuning your field. The reasons for this are manifold. Firstly, very few fielders understand how close to the bat they should be. A degree of self-knowledge is needed here. Can the batsmen take a single with a gentle push in your direction? Almost invariably. But it is important for you to delay the moment they realise that for as long as possible. The best ways of doing this are to ensure that your players are properly dressed for cricket – we all know there's a single to the man in the wrong shoes. Secondly, no player should throw the ball in anger, until absolutely necessary, unless they actually have an arm. Our team can be divided into three groups. The first cannot throw at all: a gentle underarm is the best they can manage, and this occasionally goes straight up in the air as they release it too late in the excitement. The second category can throw to a limited degree, but they require a run-up of three or four paces before they can let the ball go, by which time the batsmen have reached the other end and are considering another. The last category includes the competent fielder who can pick the ball up cleanly and get it into the keeper without too much trouble. These fielders should throw the ball in at every available opportunity, so the batsmen can see there's no run there. Explaining this to your players is one of the harder parts of captaincy. How do you tell someone tactfully that under no circumstances should they let anyone see just how bad they are?

Do you want a 6-3 or a 5-4 field?

No matter what the level of competence in your team, when setting a field everything depends on the bowler. Can he do what you want him to? Will he keep to a particular line and length? He'll have to if you are to have six fielders on the off and only three on the leg. How many bad balls will there be in the over? We've all heard the maxim that you set a field for the bowler's best delivery. At a higher level of cricket it's the right thing to do. Then you're assuming that he'll bowl a bad ball every other over. On a Sunday, this is likely to happen more frequently. With some bowlers, there may be more bad balls than good. One in three deliveries is likely to be carted. So you want to offer a bit of protection for these boundary balls. You may even set the field for their worst delivery. The other question is about your fielders. Three young, fit players can be a lot more effective than five less mobile ones. Just as an in-out field is often the best strategy at this level of cricket, so it is important to alternate fielders by ability. You want to keep the weaker ones apart, if you possibly can. Some fielders are so poor they might as well not be there. All they end up doing is returning the ball to the bowler afterwards and they struggle with that.

Relatively few bowlers at our level can bowl successfully to a 6-3 field. The margin for error is slim, particularly when the batsmen have unorthodox techniques and will shovel or inside-edge balls to leg.

But it's what is done on TV, and so bowlers persist. The better players often forget what works at this level and bowl fast, short and wide to an offside field that hopes the ball won't come to them. Playing against the V&A Cricket Club, we faced a decent quick, who came in off a long run. We were playing at Stonor, a lovely ground with rabbits burrowing on the outfield and a good uncovered pitch, rock-hard after a month of sunshine. The bowler had a theatrical follow-through and lingered between deliveries, to make his disdain clear to the batsman and restore order to his hair. It was no surprise to find that he was an actor in between roles. We had been told beforehand that we'd struggle to bowl more than 12 overs an hour rather than our more typical 15, since balls would disappear into thickets and take time to recover. But what really slowed us down was the bowler's fiddling with his field and his tousled locks. Few of his balls threatened the stumps. Most sailed high and wide. It looked great but wasn't that effective. The ageing cordon grassed a few chances, as I suspect often happens, and the edges sped for four. But there is something intoxicating when a following wind and bouncy track combine and allow you to generate more pace than ever before. We've all fallen victim to this, as that young Narcissus did that day.

How deep should they be for particular batsmen?

When positioning fielders, there's a widely held theory that they should be either tight on the single or right on the boundary. Usually this is a sound policy. But a weak fielder, if left isolated on the boundary, might fail to stop half the balls that come to them and will take so long to return the others that the batsmen have run three. So you bring them into the infield and send out another man out to replace them. Now the weak fielder dives over the ball. The batsmen run the first quickly (as you should) and turn, to find there's time for the second, as the infielder picks himself up and the outfielder comes in. They make it easily. It happens more than it should and so you hear Sunday captains all over the country shouting that they should stop the two.

The art of the quick single is a key part of the batsman's arsenal, whatever the standard of the game. There are some players who come to the crease and size all of us up instantly. The best know that if they set off immediately, there's a run there. Dean Jones did it to Tufnell and I've had it done to me far too often. Duncan Fletcher instructed his Ashes-winning team of 2005 that he wanted two run-outs a match, meaning the bowlers only needed to take 18 wickets. Few things lift a team like a run-out, particularly if the batsmen are taking the game away from you. But we are lucky to get two run-outs a season. Not only does the fielder need to pick the ball up cleanly and throw it accurately but then another has to gather it and break the stumps. It is rare that these four things happen in unison. Any run-out usually involves incompetence from the batting side. Occasionally outright malice, with an unpopular player. Your opposition is unlikely to have done much research before playing you. Weak cricketers tend to assume others are better than them. They won't know that extra cover can only throw underarm, that mid-on is afraid of the ball and that square leg is in a fugue-like state, after his third golden duck in a row. The stronger batsmen will assess each fielder in turn. Once they realise there's a single to almost every one of you, that's when you're in trouble.

Bowlers get incredibly frustrated when batsmen drop their bats on good balls into a gap, and steal a run. Even the gentlest natured have scowled at fielders who let the batsman rotate the strike in this way. But spatial awareness is not something that every fielder possesses. They can't all calculate the speed and angle at which the ball will come to them. Nor do they all walk in together as you'd like. When the fielders get it right, these singles shouldn't be there. There is a beautiful passage in Joseph O'Neill's novel *Netherland* in which he describes "the white-clad ring of infielders, swanning figures on the vast oval, again and again converge in unison towards the batsman and again and again scatter back to their starting points, a repletion of pulmonary rhythm, as if the field breathed through its luminous visitors".

It isn't like that in our team. Some of our players don't seem to wash their whites. Luminous they're not. And our pulmonary rhythm is stertorous, if not actually symptomatic of a punctured lung. At least one fielder will stay where he is, another is kneeling to do up his shoelace and a third has left the field to empty his bladder. Many players struggle with this in cricket. As with small children before a long car journey, you may need to ask them if they've been to the bathroom. In one match a fielder left and rejoined the game without notifying the umpire, as many players often do. He then stopped the ball on the boundary as the batsmen ran a single. Had he not prevented a boundary the same batsman would have kept the strike. His partner was out off the next ball. It was only now that the square-leg umpire made his presence known. Many umpires are delightful people – this one wasn't. He might have been technically correct but we all know people who manage to be right in the wrong way. He called the batsman back and restarted the over, placing the other batsman on strike. Our fielder's full bladder had cost us a wicket.

What sort of response is called for by the authorities to such displays of bad temper?

Umpiring is one of the hardest jobs in cricket. It's all very well being infallible but that requires serious concentration. A batsman needs to concentrate for the length of his innings. The moment he loses focus he'll hear the death rattle as the ball clatters into the stumps behind him. The moment an umpire switches off, he'll find he's surrounded by a number of very angry people. The simple act of raising or not raising a finger can enrage some of the most amenable people I know. Player conduct, particularly towards the umpire, is one of the great issues that faces league cricket and one reason that many of us prefer the gentler Sunday option.

We know that we are supposed to accept the umpire's decision as final but there are times when it's impossible not to question it. When choosing the end from which you want to bowl, bowlers sometimes factor in the official, as well as the wind and slope. There are some who just have to be part of the game, who are never happier than when they're giving front-foot lbw decisions. An inexperienced umpire will usually give far too many decisions or none at all. One team sent out their French player to officiate and my every appeal met with a firm "non".

Home umpires are as contentious figures as they used to be in the professional game. After a number of unsavoury incidents, including Mike Gatting's furious set-to with Shakoor Rana, neutral umpires were introduced to Test cricket. They have yet to reach the Sunday game. The amateur captain should beware the umpire who is related to the opposition. I was once given out lbw by my opposite number's father. These decisions are always contentious. I was convinced the ball was going down leg but that's a matter of opinion and his overruled mine. What was harder to take was that it was off the seventh delivery in the over. In the pub after the game, we learnt that he ruined people's afternoons in this way on a regular basis.

In another match, the home umpire had recently come out of hospital after illness. It was heart-warming to see him back on the cricket field but it was possible that he had come back too soon. He kept miscounting the number of balls in the over. Both teams were happy to overlook this but, in the tense last overs, he suddenly made a series of close calls, all in his team's favour. One was overruled by the home captain but a stumping, when the batsman might just have raised his foot for a fraction might have rankled with a few afterwards.

The introduction of DRS in the professional game has seen a great many more lbw decisions given than previously and this is, I suspect, slowly trickling down to the amateur game, though many still adhere to the rule that you're not out unless you go back and get trapped right in front of middle. One of the worst parts of cricket is when you find yourself umpiring and have to give your own team-mates out. I still remember a terrible call I made six years ago, giving out a very good batsman to a ball that I now realise was quite clearly missing leg stump. Square leg, midwicket, point and cover went up but the bowler didn't join them. I still apologise to the batter and it took me five years to persuade him to play again. In his comeback match, he made one run, sustained two injuries and dropped three catches. I fear we won't see him again.

Most of us have made similar mistakes and the dressing-room is full of the ensuing feuds and debates.

Most are good-humoured but there is the odd cricketer who will never, ever forget. The hardest decisions are always the thin edges. Did the batsman nick it or was it the sound of his bat clipping the pad? Players divide into those who walk, and save the umpire a decision, those who don't walk and, worst of all, those who say they walk but don't. We encountered one of the last kind recently. He was an Oxbridge rugby blue and seemed to nick off early on, off the bowling of a 12-year-old who'd received a late call-up. The batsman stood his ground, insisting he hadn't hit it and that he would have walked if he had. His partner acted as a character witness and the game went on, only for the same player to thick-edge one behind. The second time it was so obvious and yet he continued to protest that he hadn't hit it. The finger went up. Strangely we were far more shocked by this than any display of anger or bad temper. This felt as if we were seeing someone as they really were.

Just occasionally a dispute will break out. We've been lucky in our opposition. The worst disputes I've seen have all been in Saturday league cricket. But Sunday games are not immune to unpleasantness. One incident centred around an ageing and abrasive batsman. He liked to needle the opposition and did so pretty effectively. I imagine he irritated his own team-mates too. In one game he went that bit further. Having made 20-odd he top edged a pull to midwicket and set off for the run. As he jogged down to the other end, he started shouting at our fielder, Jon, in the hope of putting him off. We've all seen this happen to an extent but rarely so blatant. I can think of numerous keepers who shout "yes" as loudly as possible, to trigger one of the batsmen into setting out for a run. They'll tell you that they're shouting at their fielder to return the ball to them, but we all know what's going on. It's borderline at best. This was worse – "don't drop that, it's going to be embarrassing if you do". Jon pouched the catch and the batsman kept running, to the pavilion and beyond. We didn't see him for three years – he leapt into his car and drove off and wasn't selected until this year, when we were able to patch things up.

Cricket has seen many worse infractions. This was tiny but could have been resolved in the pub afterwards, had the player stayed around to do so. The final field position is at the bar. It isn't always possible to have a drink with the opposition afterwards but the day is immeasurably better when you can. They probably have their own issues with their player, just as you might do with the one they most object to in your side.

It does occasionally happen that 21 players are united against the 22nd. In one match, we were facing a remarkably consistent opening bowler. He sliced through our top order, taking eight wickets with the sort of line and length that we were entirely unused to. Waiting for a bad ball just wasn't an option. There weren't any. Every single one was short of a length on fourth stump and there was plentiful assistance from a green pitch. Somehow we groped our way to 170-odd and when their openers put on a hundred for the first wicket the game looked as good as over. But in cricket things are seldom quite as they seem. A wicket might bring two at the top level. The way we play, one can bring five, such is our mental frailty. Their opener retired with a light muscle strain, thinking his job was done and that he'd put his feet up. And suddenly the game turned. Wickets fell cheaply and their strike bowler had to pad up. He walked out at the fall of the seventh wicket telling his team-mates that they'd let him down. Now he was going to have to do it all. When he holed out to mid-off three balls later, both teams danced with delight.

It is mostly impossible to play cricket competitively and always to be likeable. Bowlers curse themselves and everyone else around them. Batsmen are vile in the ten minutes after their dismissal. But none of this lasts and all should be resolved afterwards.

Excellent advice – but was this the moment for it?

The best time to dispense advice is probably after the match, in the bar. But all too often it is done at the wrong time. This mostly happens when we are at the crease with someone, either the other batsman or even the umpire. We're taught that the man in the white coat is always right, even when he's telling you to get a good stride in against the left-arm bowler bowling over the wicket into your pads. At the crease, I've been coached about running my bat in, my on-drive (probably responsible for more dismissals than any other shot in my locker) and that chasm between bat and pad. As a bowler I've often been told off for running on the wicket or when I am getting dangerously close to no-balling. Sometimes this advice is offered in a well-meaning way, sometimes it reveals partiality from the umpire who is seeking to unman the bowler.

The worst time for advice as we all know is just after a dismissal. The incoming batsman is best off not asking the departing one for his thoughts. He's either likely to overstate the menace of the bowler or completely fail to mention his key threat. When we're out most of us go through a dark period, raging at the injustice of being out. No cricketer has worked out just what to say to a batsman whose face is turning puce with fury having been clean bowled. Your status as captain may protect you from assault but do not rely on it. A fine example of this happened at a match at Eton, when Sam was out unusually early. He is best avoided as he stomps back to the changing room. There is nothing worse than being out at the best of times but when you're playing a lower level of cricket than usual, it is particularly frustrating. Sam had been playing the day before with Inzamam-ul-Haq and Brian Lara and today he was out to some Sunday dobber, the kind of bowler he most hates facing. As he crossed the rope he was stopped by a gaggle of Japanese tourists, keen to get directions to the chapel. They then demanded a photo of themselves with the angry man. I just wish we'd taken one, too.

Who would the new batsman least like to face?

I was watching the third match in the series between the teams that Shane Warne and Sachin Tendulkar took to America in 2015. It didn't look like any professional cricket that I've ever watched. It was much more like the Sunday version of the game that I play. Albeit with a crowd. The series featured many of the greatest players to have taken the field in the last 20 years and yet the standard was so varied. They were not all the same age and that made all the difference, particularly with the bowlers. Allan Donald, Courtney Walsh, Wasim Akram, Glenn McGrath and Curtly Ambrose are five of the greatest pacemen of all time and yet all looked innocuous. The only one who didn't was Shoaib Akhtar, who surprised Kumar Sangakkara with his pace in the first match. But not only has Akhtar bowled the fastest-ever recorded delivery in the history of cricket, he was a good deal younger than the others. At 40, he had five years on McGrath, nine on Donald and Wasim and 12 and 13 on Ambrose and Walsh respectively. Watching these legends being carted around a baseball stadium was painful.

In the second innings Curtly Ambrose, sporting an amazing tassel on the top of his head, dismissed Michael Vaughan first ball. The crowd went wild but I just thought, "you should have kept him in". Vaughan had dropped a pretty simple catch in the first innings and was never the biggest hitter in his prime. By getting him out, Ambrose brought Andrew Symonds to the crease who promptly started hitting sixes in all directions. With Sangakkara and Ricky Ponting still to come, you wanted to take advantage of the stodgy England opener's presence at the top of the order. Bowling full outside off stump to him would have been the best option. But these former greats don't play like that. They've never kept a player in in their life. It doesn't work like that.

Glenn McGrath bowled the second over. He may be the greatest seam bowler in the history of the game. Ambrose is in the top ten. Both were made to look ordinary by batsmen in their late thirties – admittedly also greats of the game. An experienced amateur captain would have handled this game very differently, using the recently retired bowlers like Daniel Vettori and Graeme Swann to muzzle the best batsmen and pit Walsh and Ambrose against their fellow veterans. But Tendulkar and Shane Warne don't play Sunday cricket.

As Sunday captain, not only do you have to husband your resources carefully, but you won't always be playing to win. Match-fixing – or match management as we prefer to call it – may be the scourge of the professional game, but it is a key aspect of Sunday cricket and perhaps the only thing that amateurs do better than the professionals.

Although not every captain adheres to these principles, usually both sides want a good, close game. A one-sided match is enjoyable for the dominant players, but when the outcome is so predictable the rest lose heart and interest. They all know how the story ends and that they're not the hero. So sometimes it pays to take the pressure off for an over or two and let the opposition regroup. After all, you don't want the game to be over by tea.

There are various ways of doing this but, however you do it, discretion is key – just as it was for Hansie Cronje or Salman Butt. You shouldn't be asking anyone to underperform, nor be doing so yourself. I've never deliberately bowled a full toss, wide or no-ball – there are many better ways to alter the balance of a game. You give a weaker bowler a couple of overs too many, with an attacking field. Your cannier team-mates may guess what's going on, but the rest won't. They'll be too busy thinking about their own game.

But this tends to happen after the opposition has lost five quick wickets and is a hundred runs short of a competitive total. What is rare is having to match-manage from the outset. It has only happened to me once. We were playing a team of a similar vintage to us. I walked out with their captain for the toss and we had the standard conversation about the respective strengths of our teams, and agreed a 20-over format. One of cricket's great joys is that things are not always what they seem. But as I looked at the opposition, I was pretty sure that appearances didn't mislead and that we were the stronger side. I called correctly and put them in, foolishly thinking that it would be easier to control the game that way. We had a decent team, with enough bowling and batting to cruise to a sporting win.

I was already fretting after just two overs. Their score stood at two for no loss as the openers took a circumspect approach to batting. Chris Gayle often plays out a maiden before unleashing hell in the next over. But these two played more like Chris Tavaré and showed no signs of wanting to accelerate. At this rate we would be lucky to be chasing more than 50.

After four overs, I turned to spin, telling the surprised new bowler that I was keeping myself back for their number three, whom I knew to be their best player. (At our level, few spinners hit the stumps regularly. Each ball comes out of the hand differently. Then there's the variation the bowler feels it necessary to add, having zealously watched clips of Warne in action. The result is always six very different deliveries, which will include a full toss, a wide and one that bounces twice. It is almost impossible not to score at least five an over off a bowler such as this, particularly if the field includes two slips and a couple of gullies as mine did. Full tosses can be hit to fielders and double bouncers sometimes pass under the bat onto the stumps.) And so the opposition's score crept up but the wickets fell, too. The number three came and went without living up to the reputation I'd given him. But their number four made a quick-fire 30 and they finished on a respectable 98 in their 20 overs. Meanwhile, our two occasional spinners recorded their best figures of the season.

Half the match had passed and while I hadn't been actively trying to lose, nor had I been trying to win. I was giving players opportunities they didn't always get and they were enjoying it. My competitive instinct with a total to chase would typically have returned by now, but I looked around at my team and I saw various players yet to make a decent score this season. This could be the day they did so, if the opposition's bowling was anything like their batting. And so I put two of our tailenders at three and four. Both were clean bowled, making five runs between them, but our spin duo played their best innings of the summer, taking us from 30 for three after nine overs to a position where we needed 24 from the last 18 balls. Our youngest batsman, the teenage son of one of our players, hit a few boundaries but couldn't get the four needed from the last delivery. And so we lost. It felt strange losing like that to a weaker side but I felt we had salvaged something from what could have otherwise been an awful day's cricket.

The Tour

Every amateur cricketer dreams of going on a cricket tour. You don't have to go abroad for this. Two games with an overnight stay in Leicester constitutes a tour, and that was one of our most enjoyable. But to really appreciate the marvels of cricket, you should head further afield. The professionals may resent the endless nights they spend in foreign hotels, away from their families, clutching their Xboxes. But we can think of nothing better. It is our equivalent of the aristocratic Grand Tour but instead of the galleries and piazzas of Rome and Venice we flock to the subcontinent. The first time I arrived in India to play cricket, I found myself on the Oval Maidan in Mumbai, just hours after landing, bleary-eyed but feeling thrillingly alive. Half a dozen matches were taking place, on pitches so close together that the fielding circles interlocked like Venn diagrams. As a player, it was everything I could have hoped for. Sachin Tendulkar's son was apparently playing in one of the games and we practised in the nets at the far end, while a few footballers had a desultory kick about in the corner, waiting for their turn. In India cricket comes first. In India being captain of your team meant something, even if you lost to every single side you faced. It was heaven.

How homesick does an individual become? And how well can he adapt to the local conditions?

A tour might be heaven but it will give the amateur captain more trouble than any other aspect of running a team. All the usual factors are at play, just magnified a hundred times. Family pressure is greater than ever – understandably so. If a player drops out beforehand, it is that much harder to find a replacement at short notice. Extreme measures are required. You may find yourself having to make financial concessions to someone, subsidising their holiday just so you can tour with 11. You will also have to take on more administrative duties than ever before. Our heroic scorer, Laura, is also a travel agent, and she and I found ourselves overwhelmed with questions about laundry, currency and local sights.

Injury is a constant worry – it is almost inevitable that a player will pull a muscle in the 24 hours before leaving. On our first tour, Tony limped through five games with a torn hamstring, sustained in a net session, as he practised his occasional off-spin. It is rare that Jonathan has fewer than two muscle strains at any one time. Most recently we travelled to Sri Lanka with a sexagenarian booked in for a double knee replacement on his return and rarely has he played with more freedom. He batted brilliantly and dived for the ball in the field, in the knowledge that his protesting cartilage would be scraped off by the surgeon in a couple of months and replaced with sophisticated polymers.

As well as injury, there is illness – as much a crucial factor of the local conditions as the weather or pitches. We all know to wash our hands when on the subcontinent, and not to bring them to our mouth, in a bid to avoid Delhi Belly. But a cricketer can forget this in the heat of a match. He is shining the ball desperately with saliva and sweat, looking for swing as his bowling is being assaulted by a batsman on the fringes of the IPL. Who knows what the ball has touched, despatched time and again into the waste ground beyond the boundary? Bowling puts a great deal of stress on the body, as thousands of retired pros can testify. It is not what you want to be doing when you think your insides will explode, and you fear that your whites will bear witness to the ultimate humiliation.

Then there are the inevitable disagreements that come from close confinement. You aren't sickening for home so much as for some time away from your team-mates. Resentments build up on tour, particularly when you're losing on the pitch. When tempers fray during a match, you have to find a way to restore peace, and you don't all have a week to cool off before the next match. Selection has never been so important. The player who is mildly irritating after a match in England becomes intolerable when you're spending a week together and God help you if you take a difficult tourist. Even Test cricketers find this, as the Kevin Pietersen saga showed. You will be sharing rooms together, short on sleep and exhausted by the heat and strains of battle. And you cannot rely on victory to patch up the differences.

Defeat is almost inevitable, as the heat and unfamiliar conditions make even the best player vulnerable. The fitness needed to play cricket at home will not get you far in 35° heat. Sam makes hundreds at will on English pitches but has never reached 40 for us abroad, as exhaustion overwhelms him. The rest of us lack the technique and composure to cope with the ball turning square. There have been few overseas games in which we did not all bat. Hundreds are made against us, not for us. A fifty is cause for celebration. But we rarely bat first, instead exhausting ourselves in the field as the opposition makes hay. Our seamers are denied the swing and green pitches that make them effective in England and our slow bowlers don't have the control and skill to exploit the favourable conditions. And the opposition … Well, they are unlike any you will have faced before. As becomes painfully apparent, village cricket doesn't really exist in the rest of the world. India may be the beating heart of the global game but the majority of its population never gets to play formal cricket. Only the best get selected.

In England former Test stars tend to play in charity games or to celebrate Piers Morgan's birthday. In India they turn out regularly to trounce visiting sides. At the Cricket Club of India, in front of 20,000 empty seats, I ran in to bowl the first over to a batsman who had recently retired from Ranji Trophy cricket. We had been told we were facing the CCI Over 40s side. The batting averages were over 40 but their players weren't. It was the most one-sided match we've ever taken part in. I bowled just the one over. Against a Rajasthan Royals XI two years previously, I rode onto the pitch on a camel for the toss with my opposite number, Sreesanth. He may have been hoping to play against England that day but he concealed his disappointment well as he dismantled my bowling, and hit me all over the park. This incredible mismatch had been organised as part of the Jaipur Literature Festival but the Royals scouted our team beforehand and abandoned plans to fly Shaun Tait in – at that time the fastest bowler in the world.

It is at times like these that I wonder (again) why I am captain. When your best bowler is hit over extra cover for six off the first ball of the innings, as happened on our first tour, you know you are a little out of your comfort zone. Our first-ever game abroad took place at Bombay Gymkhana. This ground has an illustrious history, being the first to host a Test match in India. In December 1933 Douglas Jardine captained England to a nine-wicket win over India. I doubt he was greeted, as I was, by the sight of a dead rat at mid-off. A buzzard snatched it up, picking at it hungrily by the boundary. Tom, our team sage, pronounced that you didn't need to have studied ancient history as he had to know this augured badly for our tour.

At first it seemed that he was wrong. Our opening attack quickly reduced the Gymkhana team to 29 for five and I brought on our first- and second-change bowlers, not wanting to kill the game there and then. I could not have misread things more – and I have learned again and again that taking five or six early wickets abroad is no cause for complacency. The opposition had held back their two best batsmen precisely for this situation, showing a courtesy that Jardine would never have countenanced. These two put on a hundred runs and soon took the game away from us. Shattered from our efforts in the field, we struggled to make a quarter of their total.

Our next games saw us lose in a variety of ways, as we played against Osian's CC under lights in Mumbai and against a Maharaja's XI in Jodhpur. But it was after our fourth match that the wheels truly came off. We drove out into the Rajasthan desert where we were greeted by a magical scene. Our hosts had cleared a large area of scrub, brought in a matting pitch and marked out the boundary with white rocks. We were greeted with drums and garlands of flowers. Crowds of children thronged around, giggling at the sight of us, as if they knew all about our cricketing woes. The whole scene felt like an outtake from the film *Lagaan*, in which plucky villagers defeat their colonial overlords. Afterwards we stayed in a beautiful camp, where we could hear the sounds of the desert at night through the tent walls.

The calm of the desert was disturbed by other noises. Our top three sat up late into the night, drinking and talking through the previous four matches. Having played cricket at a higher level than the rest of us, they were particularly disappointed to have lost all our games. They were used to being part of a well-drilled side, in which everyone did their job. Batsmen made runs, bowlers took wickets and the fielders put constant pressure on the opposition. These three weren't used to playing with team-mates who couldn't catch, let alone throw down the stumps from 20 yards. They expected their captain to set the tone on the field, rather than being frequently at a complete loss. I can't say I blamed them for the 20-point plan they made for my captaincy. But the first rule of complaining is to make sure you're not overheard. I was fast asleep but others weren't, including our wicketkeeper Alex, who had given his absolute all on the tour. He rightly objected to being kept up by criticism of his glovework and was not slow to say so at breakfast. Scars still remain from the tongue lashing he administered.

Another tour illustrated the importance of room sharing. I had let the hotel know in advance which players would be together but I landed in Mumbai and arrived to find exactly the arrangements I was trying to avoid. The first player on the scene had been shown his room, with a double bed he was expected to share with another player. He'd kicked up a fuss and was given a room on his own. So everything shifted round. Now those who liked to go to bed early were sharing with those who would crash in drunkenly at 4am. The insomniac was in with the snorer. The tour had begun less than perfectly. The insomniac (who had been up all night, sharing his plans to kill his room-mate on social media) came on to bowl and, within a few balls, had a shouting match with third man about where he should be standing. No one likes being shouted at by a bowler but what you'd grudgingly accept from Anderson or Swann, you don't take from a part-timer who sends down three wides in his first over.

Snoring takes its toll on cricketers, just as it does on marriages. I have seen our best fielder drop two sitters while on tour in Yorkshire. It later turned out that he'd spent much of the night in the bath, so loudly did our opening bowler snore. Who should share with these people? Not the best players certainly. Maybe it should be a way of punishing the worst behaviour. But snoring is just one of the issues that will plague the tour. Your team will handicap itself in a variety of ways. You don't need to be Alex Ferguson to realise that amateur cricket has a drinking culture. Drinking after cricket is one of the joys of the game – and some like to start before, too. But while the likes of Denis Compton made languid centuries while working off the previous night's champagne, your players won't find runs as easy to come by when hung-over. Your best chance to win on tour is in the first game. After that, your chances halve. It's not just alcohol you're contending with. No one will have played consecutive games of cricket since the previous summer. So prepare for at least one of your bowlers to break down – while your fielders will resemble a robot junk yard, still reaching down to the ball as it speeds off to the boundary. There are limits to what the amateur captain can hope to achieve. I have never sought to impose sobriety upon my team-mates. If you're going to have a drinking culture, you might as well be part of it. That way, they aren't talking about your limitations as skipper late into the night.

You don't want to go all the way out there again, do you?

Many of us return from these overseas tours vowing not to do it ever again. Jonathan has tapped out – no more punishment at the hands of vastly superior players, abroad at least. Few of us are really good enough to compete in alien conditions against better cricketers and it's only going to get harder as we get older. But then the opportunity to play cricket in the winter presents itself again and we forget the shame, humiliation, defeat and disagreements and remember only the joys. And what joys they have been.

Being presented with garlands of flowers before every match undoubtedly softens the blow of defeat. Crowds of giggling children have watched us lose time and again but the laughter never felt cruel. Other glorious experiences include beating a side of tea planters in the highlands of Sri Lanka. Nick took seven wickets that day and we fought for every single run. A couple of days later we faced a side of prison guards who promised to lock us up if we lost. (We did and they didn't.) Another year, I handed over a brown envelope bulging with banknotes to a school headmaster before losing a suspiciously close game to their First XI on the pitch we'd got them on our last visit. The strangest experience was undoubtedly when I was asked after another match if our team would like massages from the opposition. We'd played a mixed team of male veterans and women. I didn't ask which masseurs we'd be getting and said no as politely as possible, wondering how Brearley would have extricated himself from this situation.

Wherever we have been we've been greeted with extraordinary kindness and courtesy, as well as mild curiosity. Why would such moderate cricketers cross the world to play their sport so badly? I have had my kitbag carried through airports by baggage handlers convinced I was here for the IPL. Why else would I have all this kit? We have on two occasions been briefly mistaken for the England team, but any confusion is immediately dispelled the moment we take the field. I mentioned earlier that there is an evangelical side to cricket and there is. National teams go on tour and spread the sport widely. Why should we not do the same with the Sunday game?

Nine months after our game against St Peter's CC, we travelled to Rome for a rematch on a ground off the Appian Way. We lost our first game against Roma Capannelle CC, the champions of Italy. The next day we prepared for our Vatican game with a cricket-themed mass in the crypt of St Peter's, as well as a warm-up in the piazza outside. The *carabinieri* watched curiously as these Englishmen in their cricket whites put up plastic stumps on the cobbles and then shuffled back into the cordon. Dennis Lillee probably never bowled to a field as attacking as this. My first ball was suitably short and wide and Tom played probably his best shot of the tour, cutting it over the cobbles and past gully. The game ended soon after that as Italian officialdom encircled us and we were fortunate to take the field later with all 11 players. Without Peter's fluent explanation, we too could have been prosecuted for playing cricket when we should have been in church, as those two nameless men were four centuries previously. We may have dodged prison but we couldn't avoid defeat. That afternoon, the youthful seminarians from Sri Lanka, Pakistan and India put us to the sword before heading off happily to vespers.

Who is Ultimately in Charge?

If cricket really *is* a religion, then there would be a supreme being overseeing it all. It's not the captain, that's for sure. Not even the incomparable Brearley. The skipper is struggling down there with the rest of the players. He can only do so much. Nor is it the non-playing administrators. Once you step off the pitch and leave the dressing-room, you leave something of yourself behind. Hence those who retire and keep coming back. Really the game is in charge, like some futuristic power system just beyond the comprehension of the player. Cricket may give you what you need to keep going, that glimpse of hope that means you pack away your kit at the end of the season, thinking you'll need it again. But it reminds you, too, that you're fallible, that your stay at the crease is a limited one. Sooner or later it's time to go.

The professionals retire first, in their thirties usually. Their bodies tell them they've given enough in the service of the game and that it's time to drift towards the safety of the golf course. Some pros and many more amateurs keep going. They pass fifty, raise their bat briefly and push on, knowing a hundred is probably out of reach. But the die-hards are still playing into their seventies and beyond. On our first tour, an 80-year-old came out to bat. Once he'd represented Rajasthan. That day he showed us that age should be no impediment. He didn't need whites to look like a cricketer. The way he held the bat at the crease was enough.

We don't know when our time will come. It may not be our bodies that tell us that we've had enough. It could be family or work that come between us and our weekend sport. Several of my team-mates have been given ultimatums by their partners about the amount of cricket they play. Each game involves complex negotiations before they can even take the field. (Another had, as his sole condition in his pre-nup, that he could play as often as he liked.) But often the game intimates that our time is up. When you just can't see the ball like you used to, and the low scores start to build up, you wonder if this is it. Why are you spending whole afternoons failing at something you used to love? The company of your team-mates can pall when you're struggling with the game. You might change clubs, dropping down in search of a level of cricket that will welcome you again, like an ageing roué looking for his lost youth. There for another year or two, you can enjoy the game again and bask in the respect of your team-mates. But soon it's time to move on again.

Some players find this decline harder than others. Good cricketers will struggle most of all. Bad ones have always known this feeling. A few will take up umpiring or scoring as a way of staying in touch with the game. Others start to contribute more off the pitch than they do with bat or ball. They know that a player who helps with tea and the washing-up is always going to edge the marginal selection calls.

Some cricketers approach every game as if it could be their last. I remember one match when we were chasing a small target and the openers had got us most of the way there. Then a wicket fell. The captain asked the next batsman if he would mind very much if the young number four could go in next. This suggestion was met with the firmest of refusals. "He's got years of cricket ahead of him. I don't," he called out as he walked out to bat.

As captain, the day will come when you're no longer sure about the first name on the team sheet. Do you really want to keep doing all of this? Ultimately cricket is about making decisions. Forward or back? Play or leave? Full or short? The captain, amateur or professional, helps his team-mates with these decisions where he's able to, as well as making his own. But the last one is the greatest of all. Do you carry on?

The end of the season creeps up on a captain. The relentless toll of fixtures in May, June and July gives way to August, when most of your team vanish on holiday. Many sensible skippers don't even schedule matches during this month. Then suddenly your team want to play every game before it's too late. The off-season is there for a reason. Namely you, the captain. You have seven months in which you can catch up with the rest of life. Come September, you are worn down by the effort and organisation of the season so far. Tempers fray, starting with yours but the team's enthusiasm reminds you why you do this and why you just might put yourself through it all again once more.

Acknowledgements

The first rule of cricket captaincy, I've decided, is not to write a book. I await next season with trepidation.

The second rule of cricket captaincy should be to thank your team-mates, for so many moments of shared joy and for unwittingly providing the material for this book. So, in roughly chronological order, I'm very grateful to Tom Holland, for introducing me to this world of cricket played badly; to Nicholas Hogg, for providing the spark that revived the Authors and playing so wholeheartedly; to Jon Hotten and Anthony McGowan for being almost ever-present, good-humoured and very funny; to Sam Carter, Alex Preston, Matthew Parker, William Fiennes, James Holland, Peter Frankopan, Sebastian Faulks, Richard Beard, Mirza Waheed, Andy Zaltzman, Kamila Shamsie, Amol Rajan,

Ed Smith, Dan Stevens, Thomas Penn, Joe Craig, Ben Falk, Tristan Jones and Jonathan Beckman for that fantastic first season. Both on and off the pitch, Laura Jeffrey, Matt Thacker, Digvijay Kathiwada and Ngayu Thairu have been heroic and extraordinarily generous. Thanks to those who have joined us subsequently – Jonathan Wilson, Tim Beard, Andrew Lycett, Andrew Duff, Oliver Craske, Robert Winder, Will Sutton, John Sutton, David Owen, Daniel Rosenthal, Dan Norcross, Iain O'Brien, Steve Cannane, Alex Goldie, Roger McCann, and many more. Especial thanks to all the teams we've played who have so generously hosted us on their beautiful grounds. Many others offered invaluable help to our team over the years, in particular Steven Murphy and Keith Gapp.

I'd like to thank also my brilliant and patient publisher Charlotte Atyeo, whose idea it was to structure the book in this way, Holly Jarrald, Lizzy Ewer and Henry Lord at Bloomsbury and Wisden; my terrific agent Nicola Barr; and Mike Brearley for his generous foreword. Jon, Tony, Sam, Peter, Sebastian, Richard and Alex all read early drafts of this book and made clever and thoughtful suggestions. Thanks also to Marcus Berkmann and Tim Rice for their encouragement, particularly when both are far better qualified to write this book.

Lastly I'd like to thank those who let us play. Julia Kingsford has been kind and tolerant during the research and writing of this book, as have the authors with whom I'm fortunate to work. My parents and sister have put up with years of this unseemly cricket obsession. And my girlfriend Rosamund has to deal with it every day. I cannot thank them all enough.

Index